EDGA

THE INDIGO CHILDREN

EDGAR CAYCE ON
THE INDIGO CHILDREN

UNDERSTANDING PSYCHIC CHILDREN

by Peggy Day and Susan Gale

ARE PRESS

ASSOCIATION FOR
RESEARCH AND
ENLIGHTENMENT

A.R.E. Press • Virginia Beach • Virginia

A.R.E. Press
215 67th Street
Virginia Beach, VA 23451-2061

Library of Congress Cataloguing-in-Publication Data
Day, Peggy, 1943-
    Edgar Cayce on the indigo children : understanding psychic children
/ by Peggy Day and Susan Gale.
        p.   cm.
    Includes bibliographical references.
    ISBN 0-87604-497-6 (trade pbk.)
    1. Children–Psychic ability. I. Gale, Susan, 1951-. II. Title.
    BF1045.C45D39 2004
    133.8'083—dc22

                        2004024367

Cover design by Richard Boyle

CONTENTS

Part One

1

Children of the
New Consciousness

Susan Gale, the program administrator at a day care center, was observing a three-year-old boy, James, who had never spoken a word and who had been labeled autistic. Every day his favorite activity was to build walls and throw things at them. He also tried to throw toys out of the window and at other children. Frequently he would run up to another child, do something inappropriate and then laugh.

However, when Susan looked into his eyes, she saw not mental illness or disconnection from the world, but a lively intelligence. Immediately the image of her highly intuitive son Dave came to mind. Of course! Dave should come for a visit and communicate with James.

The next day, 6'6"-tall Dave, with ebony muscles rippling beneath his short–sleeved shirt, squatted down at eye level with James and began to speak to the three year old telepathically. James looked stunned and began gingerly touching Dave's face and throat. Dave smiled and explained to his mother that James was wondering where the words were coming from. Once James understood how Dave was communicating, he began to pour out a remarkable story.

He was an engineer in an army, James explained, with a specialty in designing catapults. He was also a practical joker (hence, the interest in building and throwing, and the "jokes" on his classmates, guided by the "wisdom" of a three year old).

James also complained about people using their mouths to communicate—a very clumsy and slow way to talk, he felt. Dave explained that not many people in James's environment could hear words that were sent telepathically and that if James wanted to make his thoughts known to those around him, he would have to learn to speak aloud. The two young men continued to communicate for about fifteen minutes.

Not long after this conversation, James responded to his speech therapy by starting to use a few audible words.

An isolated and unusual event? Not any more. Children and young people with telepathic and other paranormal gifts are surfacing frequently everywhere around the globe.

These highly aware and talented individuals have been called Indigo Children (Carroll and Tober), Children of the Blue Ray (Scallion), Children of Oz (Twyman), The Golden Ones (Chapman), Crystal Children (Rother), and various other names that have set them apart from preceding generations. Children with amazingly developed intuitive powers are turning up, individually and in groups, at schools in China and Japan, at a monastery in Bulgaria, at a teacher's home in Mexico, at a camp and a school in the eastern U.S., and in homes around the world.

Who are they and what have they come to do here on earth? World literature, current researchers, and the children themselves all suggest some interesting answers.

Various researchers have placed the incoming children and their abilities in a larger historical and developmental context that encompasses all of humanity. Psychologist Ken Wilber has offered one excellent presentation of this wider view in his detailed outline of the "great chain of being" as it relates to humankind's gradual rise from one global consciousness to another. The Maharishi Mahesh Yogi, founder of the practice of Transcendental Meditation, has given another one that is similar to Wilber's but is based entirely in spiritual rather than psychological concepts. Sociologist Riane Eisler has brought into focus another facet of the potential new consciousness on a societal level—a culture that she calls a "pragmatopia."

· During his lifetime, Edgar Cayce indicated that waves of unusual individuals were beginning to incarnate on earth—groups characterized by their ability to utilize deeply ingrained memories and powers of consciousness from former lives in Atlantis and Lemuria. The purpose and cumulative effect of these incoming individuals, said Cayce, would be the evolvement of an entirely new level of human consciousness—a new "root race" of humanity.

Lee Carroll and Jan Tober, in their groundbreaking book *The Indigo Children*, listed characteristics of various groups of uniquely gifted children being born today in larger and larger numbers. One of these types, called "humanist" by Carroll and Tober, seems to describe especially well the entire group of highly psychic children that singer James Twyman has met all over the globe, individuals whom Twyman calls the Children of Oz. Similar children have also been seen in China by writer Paul Dong and in Mexico by Flower of Life founder Drunvalo Melchizedek.

Specific stories of some of the incoming children's real lives can shed light on the breadth and intensity of their gifts and experiences. These genuine pioneers of the new consciousness have corroborated in their everyday living what previous writers have only speculated about. Yet life has seldom been easy for them.

As the new consciousness has begun to emerge across the globe, support groups have also sprung up to nurture, mentor, and sustain the children who embody it. These organizations have taken many forms—from special schools and programs to cyberspace networks and even physical communities of like-minded supporters. Likewise, a number of specialized therapeutic modalities, both old and new, have come to light just as these children are arriving, bringing in innovative possibilities for their healing and for the building of health and balance in body, mind, and spirit.

In addition, information has been forthcoming as to how best to nurture these children and their gifts. Advice given by Edgar Cayce over fifty years ago is as relevant today as it was when he first gave it. Not only did he suggest principles and actions that are still appropriate for children universally, but he also gave specific advice for helping highly intuitive children claim and use their gifts for the world's spiritual uplift. He also gave suggestions that can help parents hone their own intuition for nurturing their children.

In organizing the material related to the new consciousness, chapters on similar subjects have been grouped together for the sake of presentation, although in reality all of the information is very much interconnected and intertwined. The groupings follow a general order that includes (1) general images of the new consciousness, including examples of real children who exemplify it, (2) real-life communities that provide nurture and support to the families and children of the new consciousness, (3) tools for healing, nurturing, and guiding children in the new consciousness, and (4) the place of the new consciousness within the broader scope of history, philosophy, and the future of the world.

2

Indigo, Psychic, or Crystal?

*I*n 1999 Lee Carroll and Jan Tober introduced to the world a growing phenomenon observed by numerous professionals who worked with children: an unusual group of youngsters they called Indigo Children. The members of this group were described by social workers and health care facilitators alike as extremely self-confident, independent, and self-motivated—strong-willed yet responsible, highly assertive yet unusually compassionate, exceptionally intelligent yet nonconforming.

Many parents could find, within Carroll and Tober's descriptions, characteristics that fit their own children. There was the bluish tone found in the skin between the eyes or elsewhere on the child's face. It was also suggested that many children who had been labeled as having learning disabilities, ADD, or ADHD were probably Indigo Children. The children were described as exceptionally bright, highly creative, and aware of what they wanted to do in the world. There were descriptions of three categories of Indigo Children: conceptual, humanistic, and artistic. The conceptuals were usually technologically oriented and were often unwilling to accept any authority other than their own inner sense of rightness. The humanists were described as compassionate and concerned for the welfare of others almost from birth. The artistic children were far beyond their years in the development of their artistic abilities in any of a number of fields.

Suggestions for raising Indigo Children included always giving choices and explanations, avoiding acting as an authority, being honest and keeping one's word, never hitting or abusing in any way, always talking things over, showing respect, and letting love show in many ways.

Certain educational paradigms were suggested to the parents of Indigo Children when looking for or evaluating a potential school or classroom for their child. Some of the elements thought to be helpful or supportive for Indigos were: positive atmosphere, respect for all students, involvement of students in decision-making processes, interesting and appropriate materials, explained purposefulness of all work done, clear and consistent expectations, ways for dealing positively with conflict, frequent praise and compliments, discipline as guidance rather than as punishment, and variations in curricula according to individual needs and interests.

Some of the children in Carroll and Tober's research were also called interdimensional—a term that could mean either that they had come to earth from other levels of consciousness or that they were from other known planets or star systems. These children were seen as somewhat different from those who had lived all their lives in the earth system—so perhaps they were not really Indigos after all. However, as with all Indigo Children, love and respect were seen as the keys to raising and working with these youngsters, too. (Nancy Baumgarten, director of a camp for intuitive children, and her teenage-daughter Llael, who functions in many dimensions, have co-written a book, *Profound Awareness*, about how to parent the interdimensional child.)

Finally, Indigo Children were sometimes seen as proof that the human species was entering a new phase of its development, evolving to a new and unprecedented level. Indigo Children were observed to be far more aware of themselves and others than were other, previous generations. Although this aspect of Indigos has yet to be researched in depth, it nevertheless offers the promise of humanity's making a difference in its own destiny—in the possibility of a planetary shift to cooperation and compassion as opposed to a future of hatred and violence. Perhaps Indigos are the children of Atlantis, incarnated again to correct former mistakes and to help bring the world to a higher level of understanding.

Where, then, do the recently touted Psychic Children come into play in the Indigo scenario? Some have considered that they may comprise the group that Carroll and Tober have called the "humanist" Indigos. Futurist Gordon-Michael Scallion, in his audio presentation, *Children of the Blue Ray*, suggests that highly evolved children incarnating today who exhibit certain temperaments and interests from an early age have come into life as part of a specific group within the "Blue Ray," as he calls it. Those of the Indigo group are especially powerful on higher, creative mental levels, for example. Those of the Green group are the loving empaths and healers.

The Psychic Children are known to have an unusual ability to communicate without words among themselves. They seem to hold all plants and animals on the earth as precious and sacred, and they continually act and speak as though all that really is meaningful in the world is genuine love. Perhaps these are indeed the humanistic Indigos, or the children of the Green Ray/heart chakra within the higher frequencies of light—returning from Lemuria as the children of Zu (Cayce), Mu (from Hawaiian legend and such books as *The Ultimate Frontier*), and Oz (Twyman). Indeed, peace troubadour James Twyman calls them overtly the Children of Oz. They have come to be the healers of the earth and its people—prepared to help raise all of humanity to the next level of consciousness through the power of love.

These are children who communicate easily with animals and nature spirits—who are specialists in using the gifts of the natural world. These children innately know how to use herbs and energies from the earth's subtle vibrations for the healing of their fellow humans, of animals, of the earth itself. They are often passionate about reversing the effects of human pollution, waste, and industrial processes on the natural ecological balance of the planet. They are committed to finding and using the best methods of healing for both human and ecological imbalances and illnesses. They epitomize the all-encompassing energy of Love, which they want to share with everyone on the earth. According to Twyman, it is these children who have prepared the new worldwide grid of psychic awareness and love, in order to raise the entire world's vibration to one of peace, balance, and universal love. This is their gift to us. Our gift to them is a nurturance of their gifts and the offering of opportunities for them to fulfill their mission of Love.

Finally, there are the newly arrived Crystal Children. They were first mentioned by psychic Steve Rother, who received his information from a matrix he called The Group. Lee Carroll has suggested that they are the artistic Indigos. Rother says that they are often greatly misunderstood and called autistic. According to Doreen Virtue in her book *The Crystal Children*, they are actually "awe-tistic"!

Virtue states that these children have mostly been born since 1995 and are calm, happy, amazingly telepathic, and highly spiritual as opposed to the feisty, action-oriented, determined conceptual Indigos on whom Virtue says the Crystal Children depend to clear the path for them, creating a safe world into which they can incarnate. She indicates that the Crystal Children generate pastel auras in the very highest vibratory ranges as they usher in an age in which communication will be instantaneously mind-to-mind, and collective love and high spiritual connection will bring about a new world in which absolutely anything is possible!

3

Real Children:
Kate, David, Faith

*I*t is definitely not easy to be on the cutting edge of a
new consciousness. Anyone who has helped bring in
societal changes of any kind can tell you that. So it has
been for any number of very real children whose gifts
are phenomenal, yet whose personal lives have been
full of difficulties and challenges.

The children whose stories are told here are real.
They have persevered, sometimes against great odds, to
be who they were meant to be and to use their gifts for
the uplift of human awareness.

Kate (in her own words)

Winding deer trails of twisted tree roots, covered in
uncurling ferns and velveteen moss, are my paths of

discovery. Hidden creeks of cool water flowing over rounded stones are my refreshment. Towering pines of strength, through which shafts of soft sunlight slant onto the musky earth, are my sanctuary. Frost glittering like Magick beneath frozen moonlight in the midnight heart of the forest is my secret.

Aside from a childhood spent immersing myself in the forest and swamps found in our wooded suburban neighborhood, my first real step into the nature kingdom came when I was twelve years old. My mother told me of an exercise she had done at a spiritual workshop on Native Americans she had gone to the day before. In the meditation exercise you would meet your power or totem animal.

Needless to say, I was quite excited, for I was positive mine was that of a red fox—an animal I'd been drawn to all my life. I was sure that had to be it. I did the exercise and I waited—waited for something, anything, to appear, but nothing happened. Not a glimpse or glimmer of anything. Frustrated and utterly disappointed, I denounced the exercise as stupid and bitterly stormed off elsewhere for the rest of the day.

The next morning I'd completely forgotten about the incident as I waited at the bus stop. Then to my absolute disbelief, a red fox came waltzing up the street. I had never before seen one in person nor had any knowledge of them living near me. The fox came within ten feet of me, paused, then turned and trotted off over a lawn and into the tree line. Amazed, I slowly sank down on one knee to get a better look. I had made up my mind to chase after it when suddenly the bus pulled up, filled with oblivious classmates, the door opening for me. After a hesitation I finally boarded the bus and took a seat.

About a year later I had another encounter with this animal companion, only in a different way that would truly unlock the door to the spiritual aspect of the nature kingdom and begin to push it open. At that time, to my horror, the man who owned the forest at the end of our road began to develop part of it. The trees I had always played among were cut down, roots ripped from the soil, trunks and branches shredded into chips. Machines were brought in to dig into the earth, blasting equipment to destroy the rocks that stood in the way of progress. The forest cried out in pain, the animals began to flee, and I went up into the woods and wept at the devastation.

I went into the forest one afternoon, walking over the shredded tree trunks and shattered rock. Sick at heart, I dug my hands into the soft earth and cried on the cliff side, begging God, in between sobs, to please protect my forest, my living sanctuary. I pleaded, promised, and bargained, willing to do anything to keep it safe. I stayed until night began to fall, curled up beneath a tree, until I realized it was time to go home and that I could do no more.

As I walked back, I caught a glimpse of something surprising out of the corner of my eye—a flash of a lower part of a fox. Black-socked feet, following in step very closely off to my right side. This wasn't a physical fox but a spirit one. Walking beside me, comforting me, letting me know that yes, someone was listening. I could feel my sorrow lighten considerably.

Within a month it would appear again. I was standing on a bulldozed pile of dirt, swearing bitterly against the man who was destroying the forest. One of my best friends was with me, and she and I had just finished spelling out "Love Earth" in acorns across the hood of the bulldozer. At a particularly heightened moment of outrage, I saw a fox sitting on the very top of the dirt pile between my friend and me. Clear as a photograph, grinning gently this time, its eyes fierce with understanding. So vivid that I suddenly stopped talking and blinked hard. It was gone. I asked my friend if she'd seen an animal of some sort near us, and she said she hadn't.

His name was Swift—or that was what I called my fox guide. Whenever I needed advice, especially related to nature, I'd focus, picturing myself sitting beside a stream, and wait for Swift to come and give me advice, which he did. Very wise advice—oftentimes things I hadn't thought of, even things I didn't want to hear but knew were in fact right. I met other animal spirit guides over time, though none were as close to me as Swift. I began seeing animal spirits around our house and in other places. I never found them frightening, and they were always very peaceful, just going about their unseen business. They were often beloved pets that had recently passed away and were still hanging around their old haunts (no pun intended!).

A year or so later I began to talk with a spirit named Donald, who introduced himself as one of my spirit guides. There were others as well that I'd meet over time. Edward with his refreshing sense of humor. Stoic Easton, whom I often caught glimpses of in his black coat and his dark hair. The delightful silver-haired Novon, who often visited me in dreams—a close soul friend. I was the closest to Donald, a very caring and straightforward character, who offered me invaluable insight on situations and decisions in my life. He never gave me any incorrect information or suggestions—and he never, despite my various attempts, gave me a single answer on any school exam or quiz, at first to my casual annoyance but then to my understanding.

Still, I found solace in nature and the remaining part of the forest. It was my retreat, a world of wonder and peace.

If there was ever a turning point in my close relationship with the natural world, it would have to be about a year ago when I was sitting in my favorite hidden glade that had an oak tree in the middle. I was just relaxing, thinking to myself, when I heard a distinctive voice:

"Hello."

It was not aloud, though as clear as if it had been—spoken into my mind. I greeted the "hello" back with one of my own, and discovered to my delight and amazement it had in fact come from the oak tree! We began to talk. I had so many questions about it, about the nature kingdom, all of which it patiently and caringly answered. I introduced myself as Kate, and it introduced itself as Elyssaye (ehl-eh-sayh).

It was the start of a fantastic friendship. Slowly I began to meet more inhabitants of the nature kingdom, everything from flickering faeries the size of a quarter to guardians of the wood three times my size. I would go into the woods every night and just talk and talk. I began writing in a journal to keep track of all the things I learned and the beings I met. I began bringing up stories I had loved as a child—fairy tales like *The Fabulous Falcon Finister* and books like *The Hobbit*.

By candle or by flashlight I would read them, and soon I was drawing an audience. My relationship grew, as did my understanding of their realm. Sometimes they would come to me in my house, in school, anywhere, to talk. I began introducing myself to the trees around my school; I'd hold daily chats with the potted plant in my algebra class since we were both quite bored. Every night I would go up into the woods, even when winter was at its worst.

Over time I befriended an elf named Chalei. When I first caught a glimpse of him, he was standing at the top of the glade, glaring at me. I gave a cheerful "hello" and got silence in response. Troubled by this, I talked to one of the guardians who was there at the moment, a wise one, whom I called Q for short since its name was very long and very beautiful but quite hard for me to remember and pronounce correctly.

It told me that the elf, Chalei, was less than fond of me since I was a human and humans had done such horrible things to the nature kingdom that he couldn't forgive them. He hated them for their destructive ways. That's why he wouldn't talk to me. I said that in fairness I didn't blame him for not liking humans, though I resolved to make friends with him somehow.

It took a long time. He was as stubborn as I was, but slowly he realized that I was trying to protect the forest and that I loved it, just like he did. I would catch glimpses of him hiding behind a tree, listening to the story I was reading or watching me when I sat in the glade and talked. Finally he began talking to me as well, and the door was thrown fully open.

A best friend now, he was my guide to the nature kingdom who was always there when I needed help. He'd even caught me when I almost fell out of a tree once. I actually felt his hands close around my arm and pull me back up to safety. He would take my arm and help me balance across icy rocks or rushing streams. But most of all we talked and learned together. I would tell him about the human world, and he would tell me about the natural one.

We swore a pact together along with two other elves, one a healer and the other also a close friend, that we would do everything we could to raise awareness and help humankind and the nature kingdom to come to terms and help one another before it was too late. I would be their ambassador to humans to the best of my ability, and they would be there with me, helping me through it all. All my guides would help, from Swift to Donald. I was instructed to write a book, detailing my experiences and encounters. This has been my mission so far, and it has only just begun, to be taken a day at a time.

David

Susan lay in bed and felt a tiny electric flicker in her womb. It was palpable: Sparkle. Sparkle.

"Oh," she breathed. "I'm pregnant."

A year before, she had had a dream of the son she would have. There had also been strong clairaudient words indicating the same thing. Now she understood the events from several months previous.

Susan lived in the suburb of a large city and drove an ancient VW beetle with a bike rack on the back. Periodically she had to remove the rack in order to add oil to the car. On that particular day she had been having an especially hard time removing the rack so that she could lift the rear hood and locate the oil cap. She looked around to see if anyone from the apartment complex across the street could help. Two young men playing basketball on a nearby court caught her eye. Walking over to them, Susan asked for help.

One man stopped playing ball and walked back to the car with her. As he quickly removed the bike rack, Susan heard a strong inner voice say, "You are going to have his baby."

That was how she knew.

Now she was ecstatic, although others did not share her joy. That was because she was unmarried and the baby's father was showing no interest at all. It didn't matter to her. She knew she was intended to have this child.

She prepared. She meditated. She practiced yoga. She made sure that she helped others with a glad heart and that she kept busy. She talked incessantly to the baby, telling him all about the world of nature into which he would come. She read voraciously on spiritual topics and spoke only of spiritual topics. She firmly believed the Edgar Cayce readings that stated that the activities of the parents during pregnancy would determine the kind of child they attracted.

She came to know the baby's schedule—when he was active and when he rested. She tried to match her schedule to his, to be ready.

Once, when she was about six or seven months along, the baby asked if he could leave for a while. Susan agreed and later found out that the baby's father had been in an accident at that time, hurting his hand. She knew then that there was indeed a bond between the two; however, that bond has not yet been realized in her son's incarnate life.

David, born two weeks early, was very confused by the white walls of the hospital. He looked into his mother's eyes and wanted to know where all those leaves and animals were that she had pictured for him. She laughed out loud and explained that the two of them had to stay in this place for a few days and then he could see everything. He trusted her.

While David was still very young, mother and son began communicating about the pictures they saw when asleep. David had terrible nightmares, leaving him so stiff with fright that his mother could hold his heels and head without his body bending. His first word was at six months: *light*. This word was followed soon by another: *man*. He was also terrified of fire and hot things. By the time he was a year old, David was talking about the man with a light coming after him while he was hiding. This went on until he was four years old.

One day when David was four, he sat next to his mother as they watched a Disney movie, *Bedknobs and Broomsticks*. At the end of it, Nazi soldiers landed on an island. Although no one in the story was hurt or even captured, Susan watched her son curl into a fetal position in his chair. She reached over to him and asked if these were the men in his dream.

"Yes," said David.

Susan responded, "See, they're not real. They're just in a movie."

David never had the dream again.

The two of them spent long periods watching butterflies drinking from flowers or birds eating the food bits that David and Susan had set out for them. David seemed to have a special way of communicating with all these small creatures.

Many years later, David told his mother that whenever he had been sick or hurt, he paid attention to what his body did to heal itself. Later, he would do the same when healing others.

Now employed in the emergency medical services field, David uses his gifts to make himself more aware of the conditions of his patients. At the scene of an accident, David first goes to the car to "sense" the seriousness of what has happened to the patient. From the residual energy in the vehicle, he can tell the degree of injury and determine what level of care the patient will require. Once with the patient, he checks the pulse to determine what the body is doing. While doing this, he actually sees the heart and how it beats. He sees the blood vessels as to whether they are relaxing or constricting. When he listens to people breathe, he can see how much of the lungs are opening up. The people who work with David have come to trust his "judgments." David sees all this as being quite commonplace and does not understand why everyone cannot do it.

David continually explores furthering his gifts by trying to develop new ways to help. Currently he is trying to learn how to lessen pain for his patients as well as to facilitate their self-healing. Knowing what a particular drug would do for the body, he tries to give the body the same message himself to possibly prevent the need for the medication. He is not working on his other gifts at this time, except for his ability to find lost things, as this is a frequent problem for him!

Faith

Faith's mother, Patricia, had prayed all her life that she be given a personal mission that would show her dear Lord how very deeply she loved Him. Once she dreamed that she stood holding a baby wrapped in a blanket. The top half of the blanket was pink; the other half was black, with stunningly brilliant stars shining on the black bottom part, as if in a night sky.

Throughout her life but especially after the breakup of her second marriage, Patricia found her faith sustained through daily contact with her Lord and also through the uplifting philosophies and messages of Edgar Cayce's psychic readings. It was into this environment that her daughter, Faith, was born. Soon it became apparent that the baby had multiple disabilities—including hydrocephalus, developmental delays, impaired fine-motor coordination, and an inability to speak—along with constant crying and frequent vomiting. Patricia merely set an intention that her daughter was going to be well and vowed her dedication to help Faith be all that she could be.

When Faith was two years old, a neighbor warned Patricia that she had observed the child's father on numerous occasions deliberately hurt the toddler whenever he was alone with her outdoors. Understanding the implications, Patricia realized that this marriage, too, would need to end. However, she also knew that at least one very precious part of the union would continue to be in her life—Faith.

Patricia worked two jobs to make ends meet. However, Faith continued to have frequent episodes of violent vomiting. Her frantic mother looked for some way to get medical help for her child, and eventually she found that the only way for Faith to have the help she needed was to give the child's custodial rights over to the state. Through many hours spent in prayer with her Lord and despite countless tears, Patricia was at last able to do this, and she was also finally able to arrange for Faith's placement in a well-rated residential school fifty miles away.

Because Patricia was determined to continue her close relationship with Faith in spite of the long work week and intervening miles, she put in many hours driving between her home and the school, spending every weekend with her daughter. Many times Patricia would bring Faith back home with her so that they could walk together along the beach and garner nature's healing.

One morning Patricia awoke very early, *knowing* that she needed to go to Faith immediately. When she got to the living facility where Faith was the only female resident, Patricia found that the previous day's aide, at the end of her shift, had simply gone home, leaving the disabled children in the cottage totally alone overnight, since no one had come in to supervise the next shift.

After making calls to all the listed emergency phone numbers without anyone ever answering, Patricia was furious as well as incredulous. Finally she was able to reach the school's director and tell him about the untenable situation, but all she received for her pains were his anger and resentment, directed at her.

As quickly as possible, Patricia arranged for Faith to come back home to live, but unfortunately this meant that Patricia had to quit working in order to give Faith the home care she needed. Because of Faith's continued chronic vomiting episodes, the children's hospital became their second home. On several occasions, Faith and Patricia were sent to the psychiatric department of the hospital and Patricia was accused of abusing her daughter—with doctors pressing Patricia to admit that this was the source of Faith's screaming and vomiting. If Patricia—who would have done *anything* to help her daughter—had possessed less strength or faith, these allegations would have completely crushed her. As it was, she was able to absorb them, fight to have her daughter's real needs looked at, and pray, pray, pray. Her prayer was always, "Father, forgive them for they know not what they do."

Measuring multiple medications, enduring eleven extensive operations, experiencing Faith's two clinical deaths—life for Patricia and Faith was anything but easy. Faith also had recurring bouts of hydrocephalus, which were eventually taken care of at Boston Hospital.

Nurses often tried to tell Patricia that Faith would never be well, but Patricia's unshakable belief in her Lord and in His overarching divine plan for Faith's life was so strong that she was able to muster the fight for what was needed and endure all negative comments. During the long stays at hospitals, Patricia always took Faith in her wheelchair for morning and afternoon strolls outside, so that Faith could experience the healing and beauty of nature.

Faith, as sick and weak as she often was, nevertheless continually smiled and smiled. Patricia let her mind go into an altered state to know what was needed, since Faith couldn't communicate verbally to say what was wrong. Autism was the official label given to Faith by the medical community, and Patricia allowed this. Yet she still felt that some divine plan for her daughter was at work, coming through her dear Jesus. Patricia was convinced that if she had the faith to wait and listen, the answers would eventually come.

Previously, while living at the school, Faith had been taught a process known as Facilitated Communication, or FC. This procedure, brought to the school by a speech teacher, involved a facilitator lightly holding Faith's wrist so that she could place her index finger on the letters of a computer keyboard, one after another, in order to communicate in typewritten words. Once Faith began to learn and practice the communication process, she relished the time spent with her facilitator. When Faith moved back into her mother's home space, Patricia arranged for Faith's facilitator at that time, Sarah, to come spend time with Faith, first at a local school and later at Patricia's home. Faith was now able to communicate with the world and its people.

In the autumn of 2002, the break that Patricia had been seeking for years finally came. Through a local doctor, Faith was given three things: a name for her chronic difficulty (Cyclical Vomiting Syndrome, or CVS), a recommended doctor who was highly knowledgeable about the syndrome and could help with it (Dr. David Fleisher in Columbia, Missouri), and a combination of medications that could help alleviate the symptoms. For the first time in Faith's nineteen years of life, the violent vomiting that had hospitalized her over and over again was in remission. She was also able to stop taking all the other drugs—eight or more—whose side effects had previously served to debilitate her functioning.

Just at this time, too, Patricia suggested that Faith and Sarah begin to explore Faith's mission in her present life. The combined results were astounding. Without the constant vomiting, Faith could concentrate on important inner thoughts and concepts. Having Sarah come to Faith's home meant that Faith felt safe and comfortable both with her longtime facilitator and in her own personal environment. Focusing on Faith's mission in life added an even greater depth to the weekly sessions.

All of these factors allowed Faith to look more deeply within herself and to bring out the wisdom that she found there. Inspired by questions that Patricia and Sarah asked, Faith began to type page after page of information—messages that she says are her life's mission and her gift to the world. Here are some of her communications:

"I would like it said that people are blocked by living—hurried up, and consuming things of no value. Everyone thinks that is life. Real life is from a point within that radiates out to the world.

"The experience of that point within is full of serenity and assurance that I am loved, that I have a role to play in this world. I am not an outsider. I am a part of the whole of life. I bring my gifts to the world, too. And this point within is like another heaven on earth. It is home. It has beautiful colors and whirling movements. It is so beautiful.

"This is the center of the real Self. It is the best place to be. If you can live from that place, you will be Love's messenger.

"You stay in that place by saying you want to do it. You keep saying that no matter what, this is where I want to live and I will not allow circumstances to take me from this place. It is a gift to other people, too.

Yes, to stand up for your own soul is to stand up for everyone else's soul, too.

"I know that whatever happens, I will stay in this state of love. That is what I tell people—that is what they need to do. They need to stay in the state of love.

"When my mother prays, I see her praying in my heart. There is a cord connecting my heart to hers. It is almost at times like a mirror. When she prays, I am praying, too. I am praying for the same things: my health, her living many years so I can be with her, being grateful for blessings, getting us through the night (because we have had some very tough nights when neither slept because I was so sick). We pray for peace and that we are good people, that we help to bring some love to the shattered world—a world on fire from fear and hatred based in ignorance.

"I do believe I chose to come here autistic. I believe it is a cooperation between myself and God. I am wanting to say God sees me as a messenger. Yes, He devised a plan to give me freedom so I could find freedom inside myself. So rather than finding freedom from the outside, I find it within myself. That is the plan—a very good one. It's us and God—us and God as a team.

"My autism is no accident. It is the only way I can function. I have finely tuned connections that being normal would hide. I could not be normal and manage what I know. The world would kill it off. By being autistic, I can protect my knowledge in the autism and use it when it is needed. Mom and Sarah are my lights on this path because they believe.

"I died twice in the hospital. I came back to be with Mom, to love her, to give her my wisdom until the time comes that we are apart, but we are never that far apart. She has loved me beyond measure. I am here to give that love back to her and to others who have throughout my destiny loved me. I have words to say, to give, to teach. To bring some wisdom is my mission. I was not ready to go. The world needs my laughter.

"There are ways of communicating with others from the heart. Here's the scoop. You have to believe—that's all. You have to be open. You have to slow down and hear—so slow down and listen!

"When I send a message to someone, I picture them in my mind—I have an image of them. I talk to them from my soul's voice and send the message with love. But this procedure of sending messages and vibes can only happen when the receiver believes in it and when there is pure love.

"When people send each other messages—like my friends in that picture [the Yale University Facilitation Group]—it is like their thoughts come to me on lines of love energy. I hear their messages in my heart, and I send back messages to them in the same way.

"I have been thinking about friends in this life who are taking time to be in a place to teach the way to go. I, too, am a friend on the path who can help others.

"Who is my support? I think my support is a higher power. I am Love, too. I speak Love and I live Love.

"Sarah is here to go full circle, to help me and Mom to gel our spiritual findings, to fulfill our mission."

Thus Faith, as one of the psychic children of the world, is indeed fulfilling her mission by giving messages of love and truth to all who are open to hear them and act upon them.

Part
Two

4

James Twyman and a World Grid of Psychic Children

*I*n 1994 James Twyman became known internationally as the "peace troubadour" when he set to music the peace prayers from all the major religions of the world. Since that time, Twyman has given peace concerts around the globe, singing these peace prayers along with many other original songs. Twyman has been invited by leaders of such countries as Iraq, Northern Ireland, Israel, South Africa, and Serbia to perform peace concerts in many places, as well as to act as a receiving rod for peace prayers in war–torn states throughout the world.

In 1995, in the mountains of Croatia, Twyman encountered a hidden spiritual community that engaged in the attunement practices of an ancient Christian mystery sect thought to be long disbanded. This meeting set the stage for Twyman to bring to global awareness the tenets and practices of the long-hidden "Community of the Beloved Disciple" throughout the world. Twyman returned home from Croatia to write a book about his discovery and to create opportunities for everyone to become the kind of emissary of light that was embodied by all the individuals within the secret community.

However, global peace concerts and the creation of a worldwide "Beloved Community" organization were only the beginning. These facets of Twyman's personal mission were designed to help achieve global awareness of the reality that humanity as a whole was poised for a quantum leap to a higher level of consciousness.

In 2001 Twyman met a ten-year-old Bulgarian boy named Marco at a workshop he presented at a friend's home in California. During the course of their conversation, Marco spoke about his psychic gifts as though they were everyday natural faculties and asked if Twyman would like to be given "the gift." When Twyman said yes, Marco reached out his finger and Twyman touched it with his. The next day Twyman discovered from others who had attended the workshop that he was the only one who had seen Marco at all, and later that week he suddenly found that he was able to bend spoons and read people's minds easily, simply by concentrating energy on them.

Soon Twyman began to feel an intuitive inner pull to go to Bulgaria, in order to find Marco and understand how the boy could appear in California and physically pass on "the gift," yet have no one else aware that he was there. Flying at last to Bulgaria, Twyman was led to an isolated monastery where he met four unusually psychic children who were being trained to use their amazing gifts for spiritual purposes.

Although differing in their individual manifestations of gifts, each of the children gave Twyman the same message to give to everyone in the world—a question, "How would you act and what would you do if you knew that you were an emissary of love right now?" The primary mission of all the psychic children was to ask this question of adults all around the world.

Returning home, Twyman wove the story of his search and the message from the children into a highly popular book, *Emissary of Love: The*

Psychic Children Speak to the World. Wherever his concerts took him, he spoke passionately about the children and their message.

During the following year, Twyman also began to receive intuitive messages from Thomas, one of the Bulgarian children, whenever he sat in the hot tub at his home. (Eventually he came to realize that water is one of the very best conductors of psychic energy, which is electrical in nature.) The Thomas messages that he received in this way were disseminated via e-mail to tens of thousands of interested persons throughout the world.

Thomas spoke of the completion of what he called a world grid of psychic children—thousands of children who called themselves the Children of Oz and who were connected with each other intuitively all around the globe. They were working together so that all humanity would have the opportunity to make a quantum leap to a higher level of awareness based in love and compassion. The message began with a specific personal reverie for anyone who was open to engaging in it—a vision that would help prepare each individual to receive the awareness of the new world.

In the second Thomas message, the young Bulgarian indicated that the Psychic Children were a sign to the world of what would happen if individuals claimed the intuitive shift as their own—allowing their hearts to expand and their energy to transform into a worldwide energy of love. Those who refused to accept the shift, however, would become confused and depressed. The activation of the grid, said Thomas, necessitated that either the positive or the negative choice be made by every person on the planet, whether consciously or unconsciously; there would no longer be a possibility of staying in the middle ground of non-choice. Evidence of which mindset predominated in the world would become evident within the following two years. If dolphins and whales (with whom the Psychic Children were deeply attuned) were seen to gather joyfully in highly populated areas, then humans would know that they had chosen a world of love. If whales and dolphins retreated from humans into unusual behaviors and places, then the world of fear would be revealed as humanity's choice.

Twyman has indicated that Thomas and the Psychic Children have asked the world to "pretend":

Pretend that you are enlightened.
Pretend that you are loved by God.
Pretend that you are perfect just as you are.
Pretend that you are still the Original Self
   that you once were.
Pretend that nothing ever changed.
It is true.
Build your life around it.
Nothing else matters but this.
The web has been completed.
Pretend you are there.
It is a simple shift in vibration.
We are waiting for you . . .

Twyman continues to receive messages from the Children of Oz. In 2002, following a peace concert in Hiroshima, Japan, Twyman was introduced to a four-year-old paralyzed boy named Koya who communicated with Twyman by touching letters on a letter board.

Koya gave a message for everyone in the world: "Tell everyone that peace is coming very soon. It will happen very fast and will be very fun. Tell everyone this so they will know." Koya also shared with Twyman a profound meditation and chant that would help individuals open important energy centers, allowing them to bend metal with their minds and then to use that same power to give peace to the world.

Twyman incorporated Koya's gifts toward world peace into a short but powerful Spoonbenders Course offered through the Emissary of Light web site, and following this, a more in-depth Spiritual Peacemaker Course based in practical yet deeply mystical methods of perceiving and acting. He has also created other group lessons and initiations for people who wish to become part of the global community of love (the "Beloved Community")—part of an irresistible energy of peace and compassion throughout the planet.

Bringing the message of the Psychic Children to the world has become Twyman's life, his love, his passion. Along with the global grid of psychic children, Twyman continues to seek out wider and wider avenues to create a worldwide cadre of spiritual warriors who wage peace passionately, in growing numbers, ultimately reaching that critical mass of energy when all of humankind will be catapulted into a new consciousness of awareness and love.

5

Psychic Children in China, Mexico, Russia, and Japan

*I*n 1990 American researcher Paul Dong visited China to look for a number of incredibly psychic children and young adults he had been told about through Chinese acquaintances—and he found many of them. Dong discovered that the abilities of these children were indeed phenomenal. They are gifted with what the Chinese have called "exceptional human functions" (EHF) and are viewed as national treasures. Moreover, the Chinese government now seeks out all children in the country who are psychically gifted and offers them special training under highly talented teachers.

According to Dong, EHF first came into the limelight in China in 1979 when a twelve-year-old Sichuan boy named Tang Yu was discovered to be able to see out–of–sight objects mentally and to read sealed writing by touching the container to his ear. This latter method became known throughout China as "reading with the ear." Tang Yu was investigated and interviewed by the *Sichuan Daily* newspaper, and the resulting article produced high interest in EHF all over China.

However, excitement about Tang Yu and his EHF was quickly dampened by a counter article in the official government newspaper, *People's Daily*. This critique claimed that reports of inner "reading with the ear" were clearly fraudulent, since such a practice went against all known scientific principles. After this article was published, other newspapers dared not repeat stories of Tang Yu's abilities.

However, members of the staff of China's highly respected magazine, *Ziran Zazhi (Nature Magazine)*, considered the stories of Tang Yu's EHF abilities to be possibly true. In order to prove this one way or the other, they set out to gather information about other EHF children from various Chinese provinces.

Among the children investigated and interviewed by *Ziran Zazhi* were two sisters from Beijing, Wang Qiang and Wang Bin. Three rigorous tests of the girls showed that they indeed had an amazingly accurate ability to "read"—via their noses, ears, and armpits—writing that had been sealed inside envelopes. The sisters told the reporters that as soon as the sealed containers came near or touched an ear, nose, or armpit, the child being tested could see the words on an inner mental screen. The image, they said, lasted for only a split second, so they had to concentrate hard to capture it before it disappeared, and the girls were clearly exhausted when they had completed all the tests. *Ziran Zazhi*, however, published a detailed article on the tests and their positive results, and soon magazines and newspapers in other provinces began to investigate and write about the amazing EHF children.

Letters from all over China began pouring into the offices of the National Science Council and the Chinese Academy of Sciences about other children who displayed high levels of EHF. Chinese scientists began to call the psychic sight displayed by such children "non–ocular vision." Other children's ability to remove, by mental power alone, small objects from within bottles, animals, or humans, became known as "overcoming spatial obstacles," and the ability to cure diseases, promote plant growth, or change molecular structure was called "electric therapy" or "external chi."

Since 1981 China has maintained special training programs for EHF children who have been noticed and recommended by their teachers, school principals, and local superintendents. During Dong's visit to China, Zhang Zhenghuan, the head of China's National Defense Science Commission (which leads the country's military research), was directly in charge of the training of these children.

Dong reported that the ten-day training programs for young people age fifteen to twenty included two one-hour practice sessions per day—in the morning and again in the afternoon—balanced by rest time and recreation. Practice generally involved "reading," through non-ocular vision, information sealed in an envelope. According to Dong's research, the success rate for the teenagers in the training program was about 30-40%, as opposed to an approximate 3% success rate for the general populace. A few of the trainees also showed talent for (1) bending iron wires within a test tube, using mind power alone; and (2) removing pills from a sealed medicine bottle without opening the container.

According to Dong, many Chinese children younger than fifteen have exhibited naturally occurring, much higher success rates than the teenagers in one or more of the practice categories—probably, says Dong, because younger children have less cluttered minds, are more open to directions, and are better at concentrating. Chinese programs for training younger children have apparently been kept quiet, and information on them has been less available. However, one section of a documentary film called *An Investigation of Life's Extraordinary Phenomena*, made during 1993 and 1994, shows chi gong master Liang Guangxiang selecting and training eleven elementary school students (four boys and seven girls) at Beijing's Guanyuan Children's Activity Center. Apparently Guangxiang has had a general success rate of 80%, and with one group of children the success rate was 100%. Dong was informed that girls have been shown to be more easily trained in EHF than boys.

Dong reported that although most of the EHF children in China tended to have their powers gradually dissipate after age twenty-five, a few of them who retained their abilities have been involved with Chinese military research as well as in aviation, technology, medicine, industries, and national sports competitions. Dong was told that the traditional Chinese virtues of modesty, sincerity, honesty, kindness, and consideration, which have been treasured by the Chinese people for many millennia, keep individuals and groups from using EHF powers unscrupulously.

According to Dong, the sisters, Wang Qiang and Wang Bin, have now become nationally known not only for their "non-ocular reading" of words but also for repairing torn cards and fixing broken china mentally, removing pills from bottles, psychic writing through mind power alone, prospecting for minerals in the earth, and healing diseases. Other noteworthy EHF children whom Dong met or heard about extensively while he was in China were second-grader Jiang Yan of Beijing, who could "read with the ear," two female students from Xuancheng Junior High School—Hu Lian and He Xiaoqin—who could recognize color and read words through envelopes that touched their ears; and schoolgirls, Shao Hongyan and Sun Liping, from Kunming, who broke sticks, opened flower buds into full blossoms, and moved flowers from one vase to another, all using mind power alone. In addition, three girls—Xiao Shi, Xiao Lang, and XiaoXu—when tested by Chinese researchers, were able to (1) view and describe items (colored stones) in a chicken's stomach, (2) remove psychokinetically from the chicken's crop all the feed that was lodged there, and then (3) remove the colored stones themselves from the chicken's stomach using only mind power. All of these tests were performed successfully.

Shen Kegong, a thirteen-year-old boy, who was called "supercomputer" in China when he first became famous in 1980, was known to do twenty-six-digit mathematical solutions in his head in twenty seconds. A girl from Shanghai, Xiao Xiong, was able to read words sealed inside a pencil case, and when the case was opened, the same words *in her own handwriting* (known as "psychic writing") were penciled over the words that had been previously written on the paper and sealed in the pencil box by her father.

Schoolgirl Yao Zheng, whom Dong interviewed extensively, told about burning holes in her clothing whenever she concentrated pointedly during school tests. She was happy to demonstrate breaking spoons and moving them to other locations, opening flowers from buds, and moving vitamin pills from a bottle out onto the kitchen table. Her family showed Dong some actual examples of her burned clothing. However, Yao Zheng's parents would not allow her to demonstrate her combustion powers because the fires had caused her to be expelled from the school she had previously attended, and the parents had eventually requested that this power of hers be "suppressed" by a knowledgeable professor from the Institute of Aerospace Medico-Engineering.

Apparently since 1986 the military and police in all of China's major cities have employed top graduates of EHF training programs for remote viewing, foreseeing the future, seeing through objects and walls, opening locks, resetting watches and clocks, and other actions—"all the way to walking through walls!"—sometimes solving complicated cases within a single hour's time. One such employee, Sun Xiaogang, a young woman who works for the police in Zhangzhou, has been doing remote viewing naturally since she was nine years old. She can also screw nuts and bolts mentally together while they are inside a sealed case, can ripen green cherries to a succulent red within minutes, and is able to restore broken or crushed leaves to their original form. Miss Sun is one of three young women with powerful EHF who all work for the Zhengzhou police. Together the three are known as the "three strange flowers." Guo Yanqin, another in this group, sees objects buried as deep as three feet underground and can physically retrieve letters written previously. The third, Dong Hongxia, can make papers come out of and go back into sealed envelopes, read words from any book for which she is given the page and line number, move objects from one place to another, turn white hair black and vice versa, and send energy into seeds for a higher and richer crop yield.

Others with EHF powers utilize them in other ways. Miss Sun Chulin, an assistant researcher with the Human Body Science Laboratory of the Chinese University of Geology, can actually change the molecular structure of materials and use this to produce petroleum! One unnamed woman, who is called simply the "modern Guan Yin" (the name of the most powerful known female bodhisattva, or superhuman individual, in Chinese history), can create halos in the dark, open an entire field of flowers with the raising of her hand, and transfer her healing and psychokinetic ability to anyone she deems worthy of the gift.

Such are the powers of the children of the new consciousness in China! According to Dong, there are apparently now over 100,000 of these children who have been identified there.

Mexico and Russia

During the last quarter-century, Drunvalo Melchizedek has gained respect and admiration around the world for the deep wisdom and personal transformation that have come through his meditation seminars and spiritual development workshops. Ultimately the information from these events found their way into his two major books, *The Ancient Secret of the Flower of Life, Volume 1* and *The Ancient Secret of the Flower of Life, Volume 2*.

In 2000 Drunvalo released a two-volume video titled *Through the Eyes of a Child.* It included footage of Drunvalo speaking at one of his workshops about the unusual children now incarnating. During the taped workshop Drunvalo brought into the room a gifted young woman, Inge Bardor, who had been trained by a teacher in Mexico City. The teenager showed the workshop participants how she "saw" people's personal situations and stories by holding a sealed envelope that contained a picture of the person. She "read" a picture just as easily by putting it under her foot or in her armpit as she did when holding it in her hands. Drunvalo indicated that many other youngsters had been trained in these methods by the same Mexican mentor and that he knew of over 1,000 children in Mexico City who had this same talent of "non-ocular vision."

Moreover, Drunvalo stated in *The Ancient Secret of the Flower of Life, Volume 2* that when he visited Russia in 1999, he spoke with numerous Russian scientists who personally vouched for the fact that thousands of Russian children were also showing the same psychic abilities that had been seen in China and Mexico. "I am convinced," said Drunvalo, "that these . . . new races of children are truly a worldwide phenomenon, one that is altering the human experience on earth forevermore."

Japan

Paul Dong, in his book *China's Super Psychics,* indicated that the Japanese government, too, appeared to be searching out and training its psychic children in the use of EHF, using methods that had proven successful in China's training centers. This was corroborated in 2002 by statements made to "peace troubadour" James Twyman by the young psychic boy Koya, whom Twyman met at a concert he gave in Hiroshima. Koya told Twyman that at that time there were at least 400 schools for psychic children in Japan, proof that this government, too, has taken seriously the psychic gifts of its incarnating children. Only in the United States does there still seem to be resistance both to the acknowledgment of and to the need for nurturing fully the sensitivities of some of its most wondrously gifted children.

6

The Place: A School for Psychic Children

Gale, the lead teacher at an alternative school called The Place, had planned a wonderful opening week in September. The older children and Gale, along with Gale's son Ray who served as an assistant, spent an entire week camping together as they visited Amish country, explored a coal mine, went white-water rafting down a river, and toured the fields surrounding Gettysburg. But now Gale was sitting on a bench beside the Gettysburg battlefield, her twenty-year-old son sobbing with his head in her lap, and the other children wailing on the sidewalk. It was not exactly what she had planned!

Aside from one girl's despair over the thousands of horses that had been killed and the youngest boy's upset over finding his great-great grandfather's grave, the others were actually reliving their deaths on this battlefield.

"We had just joined for something to do—me and my two best friends," her son sobbed. "We were standing up shooting, and then I looked beside me and they were both dead. I didn't even know—I didn't get to tell them good-bye. I didn't know what to do, so I kept on shooting, and then a little later I died, too."

"Do you know what it's like to see yourself standing there getting bayoneted?" another boy angrily demanded. "I just keep seeing it over and over."

Quickly Gale hustled everyone back into the van and headed back to the campground. The farther the vehicle sped away from the battlefield, the quieter and calmer its passengers grew. "At least," mused Gale, "after this event, they all believe what I've said about reincarnation!"

The next year, more prepared for what might happen, the group returned to Gettysburg. This time they camped directly on the battlefield. Those who had been there the year before were unaffected, since they had already dealt with the aftermath of emotions and understood that the deaths they had died there held no power over their present lives. However, there were two new students who were deeply affected.

Apparently this year the group had pitched their tents near the location of what had been a field hospital. The older of the two new boys now relived being an officer who had brought the younger one to the medical tent to be treated, but the younger patient had died.

This time Gale sat with the younger boy, who was sobbing uncontrollably, curled in a ball in her lap. In a soft voice she began to sing a song of protection.

Her young student gradually regained control and said, "Wow! That's a powerful song! It made everything go away."[1]

The group spent a long time talking, and Gale made sure that they understood the experience in the proper context. The next morning, the students participated in a rainbow crystal healing ceremony over the

---

[1]The song went like this: "Protect us with the white light of truth and let nothing but good approach. We are children of God, and God will protect us from all evil, danger, and psychic attack."

spot where the hospital had stood. At the end of the ceremony, although the ground was cold and damp, the crystal was so hot that no one could touch it without discomfort!

What kind of school was this? The Place began with Gale's desire to follow teaching methods that were guaranteed to produce positive results. She knew it was to be a place where children would be challenged to do their best but accepted for who they were. Every student proceeded at an individual pace and was allowed to follow his or her own special interests. Anyone who wished to, could attend. Many parents bartered their own time and skills in exchange for the children's tuitions.

It is a fact that most children whose parents have opted out of mainline school systems have already been having difficulties within that system. So, too, The Place attracted a number of students who were troubled. However, Gale also gradually discovered that most of these children were also highly psychically gifted. Thus, the students were frequently treated by their peers to aura readings, telepathic knowledge of current or future events, and other assorted psychic outpourings. Many of these shared experiences were positive, but some were not.

One desperate father told the teachers his son's story: After the divorce, the mother gained custody and eventually placed their son in an institution. Upset by this move, the father took custody and placed his son in a public school.

However, it was not long before it became clear that something was seriously wrong. The boy would sit under his desk and scream—all day long. Finally the only way the school would allow him to attend was if the father came and sat with him. Eventually the father withdrew his son from public school and enrolled him at The Place.

Here the child seemed calmer. Although he showed negligible academic skills, his behavior was relatively normal until one day when he jumped up, screamed, and ran to the other end of the 100-foot room. Gale walked over to him and asked what had happened.

"They won't leave me alone!" he sobbed.

Immediately Gale realized that he was seeing spirit children, and she sat down beside him.

"What do they do?" she asked gently.

"They keep teasing me!" he wailed.

"Well, you know there's a rule about spirit children. Do you want to know what it is?"

He stopped crying and looked up with guarded interest.

"Yes."

"The rule is that they can only be around you if you either say nothing or give them permission to be fhere. Are there any of them that you like?"

He solemnly pointed to two spaces in the air.

"Okay, you can tell those two to stay. The rest of them you can tell to go away, and they have to do it. You can tell them out loud, or you can tell them in your head."

Obviously he believed Gale, because he immediately yelled for everyone except for "those two" to go away. Once the spirit bullies had been banished, a sense of profound relief came across the boy's face, and he spent the rest of the day telling teachers and the other children that he could see spirit children. All were quite impressed.

Previously this child had been completely unsuccessful in any academic endeavor, but after that day, he began to learn. He was ten years old.

Gale often found it quite a challenge to teach telepaths. One day she administered an oral standardized test to a child who was particularly intuitive. In order to prevent him from "hearing" the answers, Gale began imagining a busload of campers belting out "I've Been Working on the Railroad."

The boy seemed agitated and, when asked what was wrong, he explained, "I hate to complain, but you have to get those children to stop singing. I can't concentrate with them here."

When Gale asked what they were singing, he replied, "'I've Been Working on the Railroad.'"

Since it was clear to Gale that no children were singing out loud in the school, she apologized to her student and tried to find a less noisy way to keep herself from thinking of the answers!

How did all this come about? How did topics seldom discussed in most classrooms become the focus of many conversations in this school?

The seed for the school had been planted when Gale was eight years old. In the third grade she remembered seeing the teacher standing by the classroom door, asking the children to get quiet. The room went dark and very quiet for Gale, and suddenly she heard a firm voice inside her say, "You are going to be a teacher."

She went home, told her mother she was going to be a teacher, and never considered anything else. The idea for the school's traveling format, she realized many years later, lay in *David and the Phoenix*, a favorite book that her parents had purchased through the *My Weekly Reader* Book Club when she was nine. In the book, young David met a phoenix, who determined that the boy was sadly lacking in his education. What followed was a series of delightful adventures wherein David took trips and learned the most unusual things.

The methodology of The Place was based primarily on the self–actualization work of humanistic psychologist Abraham Maslow and the psychic discourses of Edgar Cayce. Both of these sources stressed the importance of taking responsibility for one's own behavior.

While deciding on the structure for the school's approach, Gale posed the question: What will encourage the development of the eight characteristics of a self–actualized person?[2] Only teaching methods that led to Maslow's eight highest goals were chosen.

Capable of total absorption

The children were allowed to pursue avenues of study that were self-chosen, in addition to the traditional subjects. When a particular project consumed them, they were allowed to pursue it to the exclusion of all else. For example, Eli, age twelve, had never read a book prior to entering the school and had already planned to drop out on his sixteenth birthday. Through the thirty minutes of daily silent reading after lunch, he became involved in *Jurassic Park* by Michael Crichton. Three days later, he was still reading for the entire school day. On the fourth day, he did agree that it would be good for him to return to other studies. But had his teacher not allowed that total absorption in the book in the

---

[2]Capable of total absorption; making choices toward growth; believing in one's own judgment; being honest; stating beliefs publicly; working to be the best at one's self-chosen goals; being aware of peak experiences; and shedding defense mechanisms.

beginning, an opportunity would have been lost. Today he is enrolled in the University of Chicago School of Architecture.

Choices toward growth

Erich Fromm wrote that we make two kinds of choices in life: toward life or toward destruction. Borrowing from Summerhill School (the pioneering English alternative school developed by A.S. Neill) and its practice of Life Lessons, each teacher at The Place spent much time with the children, talking about making choices and dealing with the consequences. For early teens, the material developed by Martin Seligman regarding overcoming learned helplessness was incorporated into health classes.

A boy named Henry began attending school at The Place. Conversations with his parents revealed that he had been in constant fights at other schools. One day a younger child deliberately taunted him by flipping off his hat. As the teachers all held their collective breaths (since none of them was close enough to immediately intervene, and no one wanted to bring sudden movement into the encounter), Henry stood up and looked at the other child. A long shudder ran through him from head to toe. He chuckled and then sat down. The teachers continued with their classes as if nothing had happened, but later Henry was asked why he had not retaliated.

"I would have been thrown out, and I don't want to leave here," he explained seriously.

Believing in one's own judgment

"Substantiate your claim" was frequently heard when a student would make a statement. While children's views were highly respected, they had to be credible, logical, and substantiated. There were many debates with differing views, and social studies lessons had activities, such as mock trials, so that the children could learn how to present their opinions and beliefs.

Once the children were at the bowling alley for physical education. Christie was observing a repairman trying to fix the water cooler.

"Wait a minute," she said to him, after studying the back of the cooler for a minute. When he stepped aside, she reached in and fixed the problem. She was eight years old.

Being honest and shedding defense mechanisms

In self-actualization, these two traits go hand in hand. Punishment—except for extreme behaviors, after which the child was simply sent home—did not exist at The Place. Instead, the children were expected to sit down and resolve their difficulties. It was a simple three-step process: (1) each one would tell a personal version of what happened; (2) each would tell how he or she had contributed to the problem; (3) each would tell how he or she could now move forward, beyond the difficulty.

Before the advent of The Place, Gale had run an inner city storefront where the same process was practiced. There two young teenagers had come into the after-school program, both of whom were known for their tempers and were familiar with violence at home. They sailed in through the door, blithely announcing, "We had a terrible argument walking here from school, but we worked it out—so you don't have to say anything to us about it!" The staff was ecstatic.

Stating one's beliefs publicly regardless of what others think

Many discussions were held at The Place. Whether it was about a story, an issue raised during the weekly meeting, or a disagreement with a staff member, ideas were frequently brought up and defended. The older children were shown exactly how to listen to their internal dialogue, so as to recognize the validity of their own thoughts. Over and over there was the message that each person is an individual, to be accepted as-is and helped as one's talents allow.

Inherent in the ability to state one's beliefs publicly was the concept of listening to others' beliefs without judgment on the speaker. While each was encouraged to think for self, others had a right to believe as they chose. Living by these ideas prevented much conflict in the school.

Working to be the best at one's self-chosen goals

At The Place, students were allowed to set their own goals. The older children's schedule was a mix of classes and self-chosen study time. They were allowed much freedom in their written assignments and reading selections. Everyone was asked to select a course of indepen-dent study in which they could pursue any topic desired.

The younger children participated in curriculum choices, too—for example, when the older students studied landforms in geography, the K–3 children chose four landforms to study. They then decided on ways to depict what they had learned; e.g., a model of a rainforest or a mural of a swamp. This gave them ownership of their work and kept their interest. They also discovered that some of their ideas did not work, necessitating a meeting to discuss revisions.

Awareness of peak experiences

While a peak experience cannot be orchestrated, it can be recognized by the person experiencing it, and it can be named. Such was the case with Jonathan, age four, when studying the concept of "one more" with Cuisenaire rods. Jonathan and his teacher had been playing with the rods for days, and it was still little more than a game for him. However, on this day, after adding the white square to a five rod, he exclaimed, "It's six because it's one more!" With this pronouncement, he looked at his teacher with profound joy and simply roared with triumphant laughter.

"See, Jonathan," said the teacher, "this is what learning feels like, and this joy is yours any time you choose to have it."

The overall atmosphere of the school was conducive to the develop-ment of these hallmarks of self–actualization. One of the most impor-tant avenues for this was the school's openness. The Place was established with no preconceived notions about how an individual child would learn or function. The only premise was that each student was an individual and that it was the adults' responsibility to meet the child where he or she was.

This relieved the children of the responsibility of having to figure out what "game" they needed to play in order to be successful. Instead, what was expected was that they be themselves! This was especially difficult for the older children, but the younger ones flourished. They were very creative and frequently incorporated their learning into their play, as exemplified by the five year old who hung upside down on the playground bars and announced to all, "It's daytime, and I'm a bat sleeping. I don't want to be a vampire bat, so I'll be a cannibal bat."

Because each child was accepted for who he or she was, there was no shame or debilitating embarrassment. When a six year old was afraid to walk across the beam at the playground, all the others lovingly encouraged him.

Feeling affirmed, he suddenly smiled and said, "I know what to do!" Reaching deep into his pants pocket, he slowly pulled out an imaginary item.

Immediately the group asked him, "What is it?"

"My courage spray," he explained. He sprayed himself with the imaginary spray bottle and then proceeded to calmly walk across to the other end of the beam, to everyone's applause and praise.

The children were deeply involved in the planning of their day. One morning Gale asked a seven-year-old girl how she was going to spend her day. The child thought a bit and then said, "I'm going to work on my giraffe (which she was constructing out of chairs and boxes), and then I am going to research the differences between the Asian and African pachyderms."

Besides emphasizing openness to who the children were as individuals, The Place also held to a clear set of expectations regarding behavior. All the students were accountable for their choices, and everyone had to resolve through dialogue any difficulties resulting from upsets with individuals they had offended. No one had to waste energy trying to avoid punishment, since there was none to avoid! Group issues were resolved in the weekly Wednesday meetings, which the children took turns leading. Again, because there was no game to play, energy was freed for each student's discovery of self.

Grades, too, were nonexistent, relieving that stress. Children simply worked at a concept until they got it. Seldom was an older child's paper deemed satisfactory with less than five rewrites. Worksheets were returned until all the problems were solved. It also helped that the teachers themselves were intuitive enough to know when the answers were being faked.

Most of the curriculum, except for things like spelling, math facts, and grammar, were based on problem solving. Again, energy was not wasted in memorizing meaningless facts. Instead, the children had concrete problems to solve. Two thirteen year olds were asked to figure out how to hang up model planets of the solar system to scale from the ceiling of the 100–foot room. It took them six weeks, but by the time they had finished, they had an intimate working knowledge of ratios, the solar system, and the use of a ladder! Such problem solving required the use of insightful thinking, leaving the student open to intuitive insights.

Fortunately for the entire school, there was one staff member who, while not as gifted as many of the children, did understand the nature of the intuitive realm. She could explain to students the different phenomena and help them learn more. Discussion was encouraged, although this was usually not done openly during class time—mainly because one or more of the students' mothers and fathers were often on hand during classes as volunteers. Very few of the children wanted to tell their parents about their psychic gifts.

The development of intuitive gifts was not forefront in the purpose of The Place. In fact, the teachers often were not aware whether or not the younger children even had them at all. However, the older ones did ask their teachers about psychic experiences, looking for information about what had happened and how to manage future occurrences. Once a week the teachers held a rainbow crystal healing ceremony after school. Nearly all the students would return for the much–loved ritual, and a few parents came, too.

Eventually the school had to close for financial reasons. However, its founder later realized that it closed also because its underlying premise was not a solid one consistent with her highest goals. At The Place, Gale's desire had been to show the world that this way was *better*, rather than simply to acknowledge that this way worked extremely well for some children. Her desire had been to display the school as a testimony to her own life's work, rather than to honor spiritual principles.

Thus, because it was run on the founder's finite energy, rather than the unlimited energy of spirit, it came to an end. For a brief time, however, it provided respite for many a weary parent and child. At The Place, all learned how it felt to be accepted and loved without condition.

7

ChildSpirit Institute:
A Supportive Network

C hildSpirit Institute in Carrollton, Georgia, is an organization dedicated to understanding and nurturing
the spiritual life of children. Begun by husband–wife
team, Tobin and Mary Hart, in 1999, the Institute has
become an international hub, allowing individuals
and groups all over the globe to learn more about
the inner lives of children through its research, training, and partnering/consulting in related areas.

ChildSpirit Institute had its inception in a mun-
dane but unusual event in the Harts' family life when
their older daughter Haley was six. One night during the usual bedtime routine, Haley casually mentioned to her father that she saw her angel there.
Since no one in the family had ever talked about
angels before, Tobin, as any good psychologist/re-

searcher would, began to ask Haley questions about her angel. "Is she here now?" "What is she like?" "Does she have any information to give us?" He was stunned at the deep wisdom inherent in the resulting answers and comments. Tobin was even told some private information about himself that only he knew about!

Tobin and Mary then started to recall their own childhood experiences as well as accounts that they had heard from others around them. After this, people seemed to pour into the Harts' lives, all wanting to tell their childhood stories and hear about others' experiences. For most of these individuals, it was the first time they had been asked about these occurrences or felt safe enough to talk about the profound significance of such events.

The Harts began to collect the childhood stories. Using this huge file of related experiences as his base, Tobin began writing a book on children's spirituality, *The Secret Spiritual World of Children*. As the stories continued to flood in, Mary and Tobin began to realize that a definite place was needed in which the families could share their experiences and in which the Harts could dialogue with and offer support to others who worked with children. It became clear that there was a large gap between what was believed to go on with children and what was actually happening.

In 1999 ChildSpirit Institute was incorporated, and soon afterward it received a not-for-profit status. The Harts put together a leadership team from a cross section of religious, educational, research, and consciousness communities. This group was intended to cut across disciplines and religions in order to explore children's and adults' spiritual experiences.

The Institute has become a tool for researching and nurturing children in their innate capacity as spiritual beings—a perspective that the Harts see as having little recognition in contemporary society. In this capacity, ChildSpirit acts as a voice for—as well as a hub of—information. Working in innovative ways with existing institutions (such as public schools) while at the same time creating entirely new learning opportunities, the Harts seek to develop links that incorporate spiritual perspectives in education, health, and parenting.

Consulting and Research

ChildSpirit Institute offers consulting/expertise and partnering opportunities to organizations and individuals for creating innovative programs (e.g., camps, workshops, nursery schools) for children. The Institute also conducts cutting-edge research and offers support to teachers and therapists. In addition, ChildSpirit is helping to bring known spiritual practices that are based in humanity's wisdom traditions—such as contemplation—into the secular context of hospitals, therapeutic practices, and secular education. At the present time the Institute is working in conjunction with a local hospital to develop a psychological and spiritual treatment protocol to be used in behavioral medicine. The Harts are also continuing their original research to better understand the inner world of children and adults.

Education and Training

In addition to the highly popular United States Conference on Children's Spirituality held in Atlanta, Georgia, in 2002, ChildSpirit Institute conducts training programs both in the United States and internationally. These events offer food for thought as well as experiential instruction in subjects drawn from the world's many wisdom traditions.

Training trainers is another educational thrust of the Institute. The Harts have set up for psychologists and other therapists a graduate school course in the spiritual life of children at the University of West Georgia. In addition, they are also facilitating a similar program in West Georgia's teacher education department as well as consulting with both of these departments as questions arise related to the spiritual life of children. Finally, they offer training, if desired, as part of all their workshops and consultations.

Networking

One of the greatest strengths of the ChildSpirit Institute is its emphasis on networking. A primary goal of the first United States Conference on Children's Spirituality in October 2002 was to gather individuals and groups from many diverse backgrounds to share ideas, experiences, and resources. The conference brought together such widely divergent participants as religious educators from mainstream churches, secular educators from both public and private sectors, individuals and groups from the consciousness community, researchers in psychology, child and family therapists, and parents deeply interested in their children's spirituality and growth. Along with the exchange of information among these groups, the conference facilitated a kind of diversity training that probably had never been experienced before among such a wide spectrum of groups and individuals. However, the opportunity to dialogue about subjects of common concern created an incomparable openness. Many were able to bridge the separating gaps and sense a larger community focus on the very real need to nurture children's spirituality.

Another project that the Institute is working on—an enormous undertaking—is a searchable worldwide database through the ChildSpirit web site, www.childspirit.net, that will gather together in one Internet space the stories, resources, associations, and organizations from all over the globe that are related to children's spirituality. An individual or group will be able to search out either by category or by geographical area the resources for any aspect of children's spirituality in any given location in the world. Educators will be able to find other interested educators in their state, researchers can find others focused on the same subjects, and families will be able to locate both pertinent information and local organizations that can support their own efforts and offer programs for their children's spiritual growth. The Institute is working to acquire a grant to facilitate at least the beginning of this database.

ChildSpirit Institute exists to nourish children's spirituality, which includes but is not limited to "how we know." The Institute views children's spirituality as deeply rooted in two major wellsprings of humanity: love and wisdom. Without both of these, any personal powers or actions run the risk of not only being not useful but possibly even being dangerous. Any simple compassionate act is considered equally as important as seeing angels or using telepathy.

Once, as Tobin was preparing to be interviewed on a television program, he asked daughter Haley as he drove her to school if it was OK for him to talk about her angel on the TV show. Haley became quiet and moved her spine to center herself in order to attune with her angel, then told her father that her angel said it was actually very important to tell other people about it so that they could talk about it with others and find their own angels. The ChildSpirit Institute hopes to enhance children's capacities for evolution in *all* areas of spirituality by offering individuals and groups many opportunities for discovering, educating, sharing with, and supporting each other. Clearly the Institute appears to be well on its way toward manifesting this vision!

8

Enchanted Forest Intuitive Camp: Families Nurturing Their Psychic Children

When clairaudient, clairvoyant Llael Maffitt was nine or ten years old, one of her globally focused inner guides requested that she and her mom bring intuitive children from around the world together in community, so that they could get to know each other and practice living joyfully, getting ready for their later work on planetary harmony. The Internet was just becoming popular at that time, so with the help of an eclectic physicist friend, Llael and her mother, Nancy Baumgarten, set up their first small web site that included e-mail links to this mother–and–daughter team.

Eventually Nancy and Llael developed their own domain, www.PsyKids.net. Nancy tells how heartwarming it became to experience so many other parents and young people relieved at finding others like themselves on the Internet, to be able to help these families understand their highly intuitive children, and to offer them a like-minded community of support. E-mails flew back and forth between the mother-daughter team and numerous households. Several mothers urged Nancy and Llael to offer space for a physical gathering in addition to the cyberspace discussion site, since most of the families felt so isolated. Nancy queried the rest of their small but dedicated international e-mail list and found that others, too, were interested. Llael and Nancy had already been in contact with Dr. Tobin Hart, a professor of transpersonal psychology, as part of his research, and they were encouraged by Dr. Hart and his wife Mary to "go for it" with the family gathering. Nancy and Llael continued to network with the Harts and their new organization, ChildSpirit Institute, because of their mutual interest in the inner lives of children.

So Enchanted Forest Intuitive Camp came into being as a weeklong summer camp specially geared to the families of psychically and spiritually expressive children. Begun in 1999 in Asheville, N.C., it has been held in various Appalachian Mountain locations ever since.

The first summer, thirteen children came with their families for a four-day weekend, in a loosely organized get-together in a beautiful wild mountain vale near Asheville, N.C., that was owned by a friend of Nancy's. The session was designed as a family camp-out, with some families pitching their tents right in the extensive old-growth mountain forest of hemlocks and other ancient trees. Classes were held either under an age-old oak tree or in the one useable wooden lodge from a camp that dated to the 1930s. The extensive consciousness community found in the Asheville area gave Nancy numerous resources for developing small sessions, like the one given by Helen Yamada, a medical intuitive, who came to talk about using her healing abilities and to play energy catch-ball games with the little ones, who giggled and adored it. The porta-potties already situated on the land from a recently finished movie "shoot" were gratefully accepted as part of the experience. The natural environment, with huge old trees on the mountain slopes and a river running through the meadows below, made a perfect setting for taking faerie walks (led by a child with a specialty in seeing them), hiking up hillside trails (and finding there the sacred circles where many of the children independently saw or felt the energy vortices), gathering for outdoor group discussions, and participating in other spontaneous nature activities. But it was the development of an amazingly loving, accepting community in which every person was valued, affirmed, and totally supported that was key to the entire week's success. Older children adored and protected the younger ones, and *everyone* was part of the extended intuitive family.

The second summer, Tobin and Mary Hart codirected the camp, held in Georgia. Doubling in size, this gathering brought new insights to a wider range of children and adults.

Each year, Nancy Baumgarten has designed the camp sessions around the specific sensory modalities of the children participating. Nancy and Llael's annual development of specialized programs has been a labor of love for humanity's spiritual evolution. They have also been helped by the professional educational expertise of Tobin and Mary Hart and the additional kind assistance of Linda Iribarren, an internationally known clairsentient and spiritual coach (and Llael's godmother). Llael and Nancy have continued to work closely with ChildSpirit Institute and to operate under its organizational umbrella.

The first year, fourteen-year-old Llael said she wouldn't want to go to the camp unless it was geared to fun and play. So from the beginning, to accommodate this valid viewpoint, Nancy has made sure there has always been plenty of time for free play, unscheduled spontaneous activity, personal discussions, and relaxed downtime. She encourages parents to be openly mindful of their youngsters' needs and to be willing to let the children be the teachers and themselves be the students.

As the number of families attending the camp has increased, the challenge has become to find ways of creating fun for an incredibly broad age group: children from babies to teens, and parents of many different ages. Yet each year the camp has drawn more participants. It has become a magnet for families of children with highly developed perceptive abilities, a physically manifested community for the sharing, enjoying, and encouraging of all intuitive and spiritual abilities.

As the camp has grown, its programming has expanded—yet Nancy and Llael have always kept in mind the specific gifts exemplified by the current year's actual participants. The children's program has come to include such activities as a wading creek walk with a naturalist, myths and legends told by a Cherokee storyteller, past-life remembrances, group sharing of gifts, experiences in music and movement, times for yoga and chakra balancing, spiritual warrior inner work, creating a peace cloth, intuitive drumming, and mountain hikes. One of the most popular activities has been a climbing challenge course with ropes and towers. Discussions on topics like faeries or relationships with animals, cooperative games, journaling, use of a local playground, and spontaneous talk about all things spiritual are also enjoyed. Specialized opportunities are made available for such experiences as interactively studying the life force, healing with energy, enjoying dowsing, playing deep empathy games, participating in chi gong exercises, exploring how to put out intentions into the world, and working with art and dreams.

Whole-group activities have included such events as group hikes; a swimming trip to a beautiful mountain lake; a spiritual ecotour of a forest, sacred cave, and waterfall; fishing for trout for supper; creating Genesa forms for balancing and activating energy fields; paddling on a pond; creating a camp yearbook; and celebrating through rituals, with a new moon ceremony for girls and women, and a spiritual warrior ceremony for boys and men.

Parents are offered their own group discussions and workshops on such subjects as ancient wisdom schools and their relation to today's intuitive children, metaphysical parenting, the importance of service to others, awakening cellular memory, family supersensory emergencies, multidimensional sensory integration, yoga and chi gong, and educational brainstorming. Knowledgeable facilitators are always available for individual or group discussions of pertinent issues and for support or information on countless topics: angels, faeries, spirits, astral travel, auras, healing energy fields, dowsing, etc.

In 2002 the decision was made to suspend 2003 camp activities until the summer of 2004. This choice was made primarily to allow time for Nancy and Llael to finish their book manuscript and also to give the Harts, Nancy, and the fourth member of the team—master intuitive and business consultant Linda Iribarren—a chance to reassess and incorporate into the existing program their joint vision of a new paradigm of learning. Using this, they intend to develop a distance–learning program for the "education of the spirit" and to offer to a wider group of communities the information and expertise to create their own local and regional camps, as well as other programs for children with heightened perception. Nancy and Llael's coauthored book on parenting the multidimensional child—*Profound Awareness*—has also resulted from this timeout, adding further to the information available to parents and children for experiencing their human birthright of wider, more complete forms of perception.

Thus not only the national Enchanted Forest Intuitive Camp, but also multiple regional and local camp experiences in 2004 and beyond promise even greater potential for nurturing children's supersensory and mystical abilities through the common vision of all those who would both plan and participate in their supportive programs.

9

Nova High School: A Partnership Community

❧

*I*n her recent book, *Tomorrow's Children*, Riane Eisler has painted a picture of what she sees happening in today's world that is genuinely leading toward a true partnership society. One of the real–life examples that Eisler offers is that of students at a thriving high school located in Seattle, Washington: Nova High School.

In Eisler's earlier book, *The Chalice and the Blade*, she listed the marks of a partnership society as (1) an emphasis on egalitarianism, (2) peaceful technologies that remove the worldwide necessity for such events as famine and war, (3) values that stress interconnectedness, cooperation, trust, and caring among individuals and communities, and (4) a reverence for nature. All of these can be found in the organization and curriculum of Nova High School.

Nova was begun in 1970 by a group of teachers and students as an alternative high school in the Seattle area. According the school's web site, www.novaproj.org, Nova currently offers a wide variety of unique courses and a democratically run school government in which students and teachers contribute equally to the decision–making process. The 265 students who presently make up the student body at Nova participate actively in their own curricula and classes. The school is governed by faculty–student committees in which both staff and students have equal membership status. Teachers on the committees act as role models for students, and students who serve as members learn leadership, responsibility, and group relationship skills. All decisions are made by consensus.

Each staff member serves as a coordinator for those students who have chosen him or her as their mentor. The school web site states that coordinators offer personal counseling and academic advising, help with college selection and application, and give general support and encouragement for the students who have chosen to work with them. The coordinators also act as their students' liaison to other teachers, to parents, and to admission personnel at colleges.

Credits for classes at Nova are based on a written contract system between students and teachers. Classes may be taken for credit or no-credit, and grades are simply "pass." "Pass" infers an 80% mastery level in any subject. According to the school web site, Nova offers a wide range of classes, from a comprehensive science program complete with an organic garden, to history, language arts, advanced math, French, Spanish, peer mediation, photography, digital video production, web design, audio recording, computer labs, desktop publishing of a newsletter and literary zines, drama productions, internships, and foreign exchanges.

Nova is proud of its sense of community, which students and faculty alike consider fundamental to the learning process as well as to the enhancement of personal responsibility and group cooperation. According to the Nova web site, this sense of community has emerged from the caring attitudes of everyone involved. Special events, such as weeklong backpacking hikes organized by individual teachers, help to create interpersonal bonds and cooperative learning in ways that go far beyond ordinary academic class interaction.

Application to Nova is by choice. The school web site states that some students have come to Nova because they did not receive sufficient stimulation or range of choice at other institutions. Others "failed" in previous schools due to academic, personal, or social factors. Nova students are of mixed racial and ethnic origins, many are from poor families, and some are even from homeless families. Participants at Nova especially enjoy the atmosphere of acceptance and the diversity inherent in its broad range of participants. Students are sensitive to and empowering of each other and their individual gifts.

Riane Eisler has helped facilitate the school's curriculum, which is based on her partnership societal model. Thus far this educational model has shown excellent results. Nova has been ranked first in Seattle's high schools in educational climate, its students have scored very well on standardized assessment tests, and a high percentage of its graduates have been accepted at a wide variety of colleges and universities, including prestigious institutions. Eisler indicates that because all students are empowered by Nova's egalitarian organizational structure and emphasis on respect and mutual caring, they are able to free up amazing energies for learning, creativity, and cooperative growth.

Nova's web site states that the school has had a remarkable impact on its students' lives, motivating them to personal growth and responsible community leadership. Students and faculty together continue to experiment with innovative educational methods and content, including a plan for students to gain graduation credits through demonstrated competencies, portfolios, and committee presentations.

In addition to Nova, Eisler mentions other schools that model the partnership way, including La Escuela Fratney, a democratic bilingual public elementary school in Milwaukee, Wisconsin; The School in Rose Valley (Pa.); and many individual educational institutions worldwide that are based on Maria Montessori's methods. In *Tomorrow's Children*, Eisler outlines a curriculum for all ages that partnership schools of the future can utilize. She describes such a school as "a place of adventure, magic, and excitement, a place that, generation after generation, adults will remember from their youth with pleasure . . . " and she says that schools around the world—in such places as Australia, Israel, Germany,

Greece, South Africa, Hungary, the Philippines, Italy, and Sweden—are beginning to experiment with democratic, cooperative educational methods. In addition, Eisler's own Center for Partnership Studies (informally known as CPS) is collaborating with numerous schools, universities, and other organizations to further develop processes, structures, and curricula that reflect the partnership way.

Eisler is well aware that bringing partnership education to the entire planet is an ambitious goal. However, evidence suggests that educational systems around the globe are already beginning to move, even if slowly, toward the attitudes and methods that will be needed in order to empower the incoming new wave of children. It is that empowerment that has the potential of eventually bringing about a global shift in the entire consciousness of humanity.

10

A Place of Light: A Community Center for Intuitive Children

*P*eggy and Susan had each spent over fifty years in this lifetime preparing for the beginning of A Place of Light. Each knew she was getting ready for some important future event, but neither knew exactly what it would be.

Susan's preparation had begun with the parents she chose. Her father was a natural teacher, making everything relevant to her immediate experience— taking the time to talk, explaining things, listening to her questions, and using a sense of humor to soften all criticisms. Her mother taught her to keep both feet firmly on the ground and to do her homework before beginning any task. Both parents instilled the foundation of doing one's best in whatever task one undertook.

Almost all of Susan's early teaching experiences were with children who were suffering distress of some sort. These youngsters taught her much about how one could learn when removed from stifling methodologies. Gradually in her studies she discovered methods for nonviolent conflict resolution and steps for counteracting learned helplessness. As she studied the wisdom of Abraham Maslow and Edgar Cayce, she learned how to structure learning environments so as to bring out the characteristics in children that would create positive emotional health.

When Susan found that mainstream educators were not interested in her approach, she began to develop programs of her own. Although all of these programs were successful for children and staff, Susan was still looking for ways to work with those who, to her, seemed blind as to how children should be treated. Gradually, in developing numerous programs over many years, she eventually acquired a deep knowledge of highly workable ways to create, organize, and administer environments that could engender positive emotional health in children and staff. She gave countless workshops on this topic to professionals in schools, camps, and early childhood programs.

Throughout this professional development, Susan also worked on her spiritual life, especially as guided by the *Search for God* material from the Edgar Cayce readings. The fact was that no matter what hardship she faced, these premises held true. This strengthened Susan's beliefs and gave her the wisdom and power to move through all adversities that came her way. She openly spoke of psychic phenomena to everyone she met.

Yet, as she drifted from one job to another, she knew she was not fulfilling her life's plan. It was clear to her that she was not going to be allowed to stay at any one job until she found the right place. Finally, at one point she e-mailed the Association for Research and Enlightenment and asked for the name of someone who was interested in working with psychic children. She was given Peggy's name.

Immediately she e-mailed Peggy and found a wonderfully supportive woman who shared many of her interests. Then one day there came the e-mail she had been waiting for years to see. Its subject line said: *How about starting a school in a year or two?*

Peggy, meanwhile, had spent childhood in her own land of daydreams, not realizing that this realm was not even acknowledged by most people or, at best, was considered quite different from the "real", world of siblings, parents, church, and school. However, her parents were lovingly tolerant of their quiet, "moony" daughter, allowing all their children great freedom of action and choice, yet keeping strict boundaries on behavior through family routines and expectations.

Peggy was always fascinated with young children, yet overwhelmed by their energy if she was with more than one at a time. After a year of public school teaching, in which she tried to coach each child personally, she finally left the classroom to raise her own family and tutor individual students. As her daughter and son matured, Peggy spent more time with them in creative pursuits—sewing, writing, cooking, designing, gardening, playing and listening to music, walking in the woods. She became passionate about learning to meditate. She encouraged her children's individual gifts. When her youngest left home for college and her husband began working in New York City on weekdays, Peggy found herself with unlimited free time to pursue whatever she wished.

At this very point in time, Peggy received a member letter from the Youth and Family Life Department of the Association for Research and Enlightenment, asking for a volunteer to help compile a parenting handbook based on principles found in the psychic readings of Edgar Cayce. Here was Peggy's opportunity to combine her love of children with the goals of a spiritual organization, at the same time utilizing the kind of research that had been her greatest joy in school. It was a match made in heaven.

Eventually the project was finished, but not before Peggy had begun to realize how important all its elements were to her: children, spirituality, and independent creative thinking. Again combining all these factors, Peggy completed her master's degree in transpersonal studies. The very week of her graduation, she received an e-mail from Susan asking if she were interested in working in some way with psychic children. Of course, she was—it would involve again that same magic, that same combination of children, spirituality, and creativity! And she would have an *exceptionally* knowledgeable partner to work with!

That was the beginning. The energy was so high that it crackled. The

e-mails flew back and forth, each one carrying new suggestions of possibilities—ideas, images, plans. Finally the two women met in person
and began spending hours each week poring over possible sites and
talking about atmosphere and classes, budgets and brochures, business
organization and spiritual intentions. Almost everything seemed to fall
into place easily—except the building itself.

The search for just the right building took weeks and weeks. Finally,
just as Susan and Peggy were beginning to get discouraged, both women
came to an amazing awareness: as long as either one's own personal
preferences were being put in first place above the purely spiritual intention simply to help children in the best ways possible, neither the
building nor the children would be forthcoming.

At four o'clock one morning, Peggy and Susan, both of them barely
awake yet fully aware that their joint intention must be *totally* open to
being led by Spirit alone, logged onto a computer and were shown
exactly the right house for a small program center for psychic children.
Since that time, amazing things have happened.

The concept of A Place of Light is a simple one: the provision of a safe
haven where children can explore their creative gifts as well as their
intuitive ones. The emphasis is on community rather than psychic development. While there are some classes on intuitive abilities, the program primarily offers a setting wherein children can freely use and
discuss their gifts. Parents are also welcome to join in the classes, for
with parental support and involvement the programs are far more effective. In fact every attempt is made to sit down with the parents and
children prior to enrollment so that everyone has a clear vision of what
will be happening.

The classes are based in discovery rather than information–giving.
There are no teachers in the traditional sense. At A Place of Light, the
leader's primary responsibility is to create an environment wherein
knowledge, wisdom, and talents can be shared, discovered, and cel-
ebrated. All contribute to the learning process, which is truly a problem–solving process. No one is expected to have all the answers,
including the leader.

The program offers activities that can help intuitive children develop
their gifts: sending and receiving messages, using crystals, reading sym-

bols. The children have opportunities to engage in activities that encourage the use of their creativity: drama, writing, storytelling, art. Also, in keeping with suggestions from the Edgar Cayce readings, much attention is paid to the natural world in order for the children to understand how it operates and how human beings fit into the larger context of life.

A Place of Light also offers a development workshop for teachers, "The Classroom of Compassion." This seminar is designed to assist teachers in creating a classroom culture that effectively facilitates nonviolent behavior. Support groups provide the needed follow-up dialogue for the application of these concepts.

In addition to providing expanded afternoon and evening programs, A Place of Light is making long-range plans for developing first a children's traveling day camp during the summer and then a K-twelve school where children's intuitive gifts will be tapped in studying ordinary subjects. To peer into the inner workings of a cell or to experience history through their psychic knowing will enable them to experience a kind of richness a textbook or lecture will never provide.

Within the humble hillside building that houses A Place of Light, a rich and supportive community is developing. Here people of all ages are able to speak freely of their gifts while carrying on with everyday life events. We play, study, and laugh as we all seek to know that still, small voice that is present to guide us all.

11

EarthWalk: Empowering Highly Aware Families

by Valerie Thea Vandermeer,
EarthWalk Founder

How we hunger for understanding! It seems as though it is programmed into our human brains to make order and create sense out of the world around us. This is the thing I notice the most about myself and other parents with highly aware children. We try to explain what they are doing and how. We try to understand them by the color of their aura or their place in an energetic hierarchy. We search in vain for guidance, information, direction—seeking the holy grail of conscious parenting. We use very sophisticated metaphysical language to mask our inner hunger for comprehension. But when laid bare, it is essentially the same urge of parents everywhere: to understand and do the best they can for their children.

These new children populating the earth are indeed all extraordinary, but they are not all alike. They exhibit a tremendous range and degree of abilities and awareness. There is no single path for parenting them, no one book that can illuminate our daily challenges, no experts to guide us. This is so for a very important reason. Our children are deeply self-referenced. They feel and intuitively know who they are and they are expecting us as their parents to be like them. They challenge us to let go of our left-brain fascination with acquiring answers and immerse ourselves instead in the first-person immediacy of experience and inner wisdom.

How to do this? How do I let go of my idea about my child and instead be fully present in the everyday experience of the rich and diverse layers of her being? That was the question tugging at the edges of my very rational brain at three in the morning. I sat in a dimly lit hall outside my hotel room and stared at a yellow pad of paper. Moments later my pen began to race across the pad. A decade of experience with healing, shamanism, and human nature blended with the insights I had gained parenting my own highly aware child and just like that, EarthWalk was born.

Of course, the seed had been planted all those years earlier. It began with my first healing class. I reached out my seemingly ordinary hands into the energy field of my practice client and, with a single gesture of visceral inquiry, fundamentally altered my perception of my self and the nature of reality. My hands reached out to touch a human body, but instead they entered a galaxy of stars pulsing with unimaginable power and extraordinary light. In that instant I understood that we humans are literally formed of palpable magic.

In the ensuing weeks my sense of wonder grew through this process of healing touch. I couldn't help but imagine how the world would change if everyone could have an opportunity to experience what I did just once; if everyone could literally feel how amazing it is to be alive and in a human body. How easy it would be to feel deep reverence for life once you'd reached out and touched its essence. How easy it would be to trust yourself, once you'd glimpsed your connection to all the answers. Along with these musings, an insistent thought kept pressing itself into my consciousness: "Every teacher of young children must experience this." I knew that what I had experienced was central to unlocking human potential. It felt essential that people working with children encounter this level of empowerment. It would be a path for transforming humanity.

Those thoughts whispered within the inner recesses of my mind for thirteen years. Then they emerged one day, as I was typing out some of the EarthWalk ideas:

A Call to the Deep-Hearted
Healers and Teachers

As deep-hearted healers and teachers, we know that humanity and the world we inhabit are changing. Our challenge is to continue to share our gifts through the flux and flow of emergence—through the development of an entirely new way of being. As our world culture shifts to an entirely new paradigm—or to no paradigm at all—we as healers and teachers must allow our methods and tools to evolve as well. This is particularly so in our work with all children, and acutely so when working with the many Highly Aware children who now walk amongst us.

There was the answer, the way to do it—let go of the paradigm. Let go of the healing paradigm. Let go of the shamanism paradigm. Let go of the parenting paradigm. I suddenly realized why so many people's genuine and kind attempts at helping these children had left me feeling frustrated. Their approaches were lodged in deeply held metaphysical beliefs. Even though they were good beliefs, together they formed a kind of new-age dogma. The very ideas that had set my spiritual contemporaries and me free and had served us so well were now restrictive in the light of the incredible emerging consciousness available to all beings now. The concept of unlimited potential has found a home in our children. It is now a multidimensional actuality that challenges us all to drop ideas, systems, and concepts and move into deeply authentic personal experience. We must reach for our inner wisdom.

That is what these children show us every day. They remember the truth of what it is to be alive, the potent magic of our beings. They retain their connection to all wisdom and therefore trust themselves as utterly wise. They do not hold these as ideas or as mental constructs about who they are; they simply are. They pose an extraordinary challenge for us all—not because of what they are capable of, but because we are *all* capable of this level of being right now. This is the heart of the EarthWalk approach—the empowerment of highly aware families so that they can move into deeply authentic relationship and experience more joy and aliveness in this dance of life.

EarthWalk provides support, guidance, and programs to help these highly aware children and their families better understand and appreciate their multisensory and multidimensional abilities. We teach them practical tools for living in wholeness, harmony, and joy, and for embracing their path of being in a body, walking on this earth, now. We invite them to flourish in their role as stewards of a new level of human consciousness. EarthWalk families aren't out in the world looking for answers; they are deep in their hearts finding them.

As children, we were all aware to one degree or another. But for most of us at some juncture in our growing up, we learned to veil the magic within us. Some shut it down entirely. Others masked it or named it imagination. Some managed to express it through art or other creative acts. Very few of those who are parents today were able to maintain, develop, and nurture their innate awareness and inherent magic as children. I have found that difficulties most often begin when a highly aware child reaches the age at which the parent's own awareness started to shut down. When adults are taught how to recover and repair those early insults to awareness, they become deeply and powerfully present in their role as parents.

At EarthWalk Retreats, parents and children are all immersed in experiences together. If the kids are coloring energy pictures with crayons, then the parents are on the floor with them doing the very same thing. By engaging in these activities side by side as peers, parents deepen their empathy and can better appreciate how their highly aware child perceives and relates to the world. It also gets them out of thinking mode and into being, which can help to highlight the areas of discomfort or resistance that are creating energetic roadblocks to effective parenting. A parent could be quite comfortable about blindly reaching into a bucket of crayons, trusting their hand to select just the perfect color to use. But that same parent might crumble in a group in which everyone is invited to call out his or her name in joyful self-expression. These unconsciously held beliefs can be quite easy to recognize.

Recognition is only the first step, though. We teach our families simple techniques of visualization, bodywork, and breathing so that they can change old ideas and embody new thoughts. We don't do these things for them; we teach them how to do it for themselves. The techniques have been removed from any metaphysical paradigms and have been reanimated as totally open-ended, self-directed processes. I have witnessed adults make dramatic and lasting change through these methods, and the children thrive on this approach. Highly aware children are brilliant at seeing and articulating a problem and then coming up with their own ideas for finding resolution. We just have to remember to ask them in a way that allows them to feel empowered. Open-ended questions like, "Can you imagine a way to support yourself in this problem?" or "What can you do to create more safety for yourself?" open doorways to their incredible inner resources.

Deeply authentic parenting is a leap of faith into the unknown. When we let go of all the pat answers and preconditioned responses, we can be truly present with our children. One of the greatest challenges in putting together the EarthWalk program was in making that same leap, both in myself as a teacher and in the actual structure of the program. We don't do processes or exercises as in a traditional workshop approach. We play—and in the context of play we invite participants into what we have termed "experiences." An EarthWalk experience is an event or activity that invites participants to become aware of themselves in a new context. For example, we all know and say our names daily, but we are able to freshly perceive our identity and ourselves when we call out our name loudly and exuberantly in the surroundings of nature. In planning the Retreat, we develop many of these different experiences, but we do not know which ones will be used. We completely trust that the children will let us know, in subtle and overt ways, which experiences they choose for their learning. We are also prepared to change direction and spontaneously cocreate new experiences.

Anyone who has spent any time with a highly aware child will tell you that that child can sense integrity. He or she can get quite disturbed in the presence of people who think one thing and say another. This can be very challenging for parents who are accustomed to telling "little white lies" or are unaware when their own thoughts and actions are at odds with each other. Such behaviors can create a constant subtle stressor in a home with a highly aware child. Many of these children can literally read minds, and all of them are adept at receiving the energy of thoughts in varying degrees. When thoughts and words don't match, it can be extremely confusing and unsettling to these children. At EarthWalk Retreats, we adopt a twenty–four–hour integrity policy and request participants to do the same. This allows the children to begin relaxing the defenses that some of them build up when "out in the world." As teachers/learners, we must be completely willing to share our true feelings and reactions. We openly model for the families the methods we use ourselves for personal change and growth. As they observe us and how the children respect and respond to this level of authenticity, they can become empowered to open themselves more as parents.

Highly aware children are masters of energy, but being fully present in their earthly bodies can often pose a challenge. I noticed a lot of programs for these children responding to the children's ethereal qualities with equally ethereal programming. EarthWalk goes in a different direction. We want to help these kids to feel the joy of body ownership and embrace their chosen path of walking on the earth. We want them to be able to fully experience the fruits of their multidimensionality within their bodies. We invite our participants to experience their bodies as magical instruments which empower rather than limit their spiritual essence. But we balance this with a program that honors and acknowledges their incredible capacity to be energetically connected to each other and to other beings around the planet.

One way we do that is through our Love Sharer program. Some extraordinary healers have volunteered to support EarthWalk kids and families by opening their hearts and spiritual energy to them for a specific period of time. They offer their love lesson via heart-to-heart delivery. There is no written or physical contact. The support and learning comes from the intentional vibration of pure love. They teach by being—we learn by receiving. At EarthWalk Retreats, energetic connections are again reinforced with the Heart-to-Heart Kids project which invites participants to keep in touch with one another on both the physical and energetic planes. We also share with participants some specific techniques related to this spiritual/physical balance. For example, when you ask a highly aware child to do something, it can be most effective if you first create a mental picture of what you want to happen, *before* you state the words that go with that inner image. This helps them to be more fully integrated in their communications.

One important aspect of empowering families is bringing them together and encouraging them to make their own connections and provide support to one another. It is vital that these children find one another and have time to play with and just be with each other. So many parents feel isolated or find it difficult to relate to other families. A family can choose to sponsor an EarthWalk Retreat as a way to form connections with other highly aware families. When I planned the first Retreat in my area, we instantly acquired several new local playmates for my daughter. ListServes are established for each Retreat region so that parents can connect easily. The ListServes are driven by the same principles that inform EarthWalk: as spiritual beings, we are ultimately wise, and our children are able to draw to themselves the experiences they require for their learning. As families become more empowered, we envision them creating local initiatives to raise awareness of consciousness and connection for all children—for it is through learning how to serve our highly aware children that we gain critical insights into how all human beings are meant to treat one another.

The original response to EarthWalk was instantaneous and astounding. In a few short months it grew from a simple idea and a web site (www.earth-walk.net) to several Retreats and requests from families in cities all across the U.S. We've launched a new paradigm school initiative with local EarthWalk families and developed a training program for professionals who'd like to learn the EarthWalk approach for working with highly aware children. Ultimately the vision calls for a shift from highly aware to highly aware everywhere, as more and more people wake up to their own inherent gifts and abilities.

There is no doubt that our highly aware children are extraordinary and exquisite beings. They are to be treasured as the harbingers of magnificent evolutionary change. But it is easy to become fascinated with their magnetic energy and remarkable wisdom. When we do, we forget that they are here to teach us that *we are all dazzling beings of light*. Each of us is blessed by being present on the planet, experiencing the magic and joy of aliveness. This is what they ask us to remember and this is what they invite us to embody in our own EarthWalk.

12

Vedic City, Iowa:
One Prototype for Society

*I*n 1988 the Maharishi Mahesh Yogi announced the initiation of a broad program which he called the "Master Plan to Create Heaven on Earth." It had originated with the Maharishi's Transcendental Meditation (TM) and later his *sidhi* program, but the newly expanded program proposed broad new societal and cultural structures that would facilitate both the inner growth and the outer life of as many individuals as possible around the globe. Many of the proposed structures were to begin in a model city that would be built according to, and governed by, the teachings of ancient Vedic literature from India. In July of 2001 Vedic City, Iowa, became an incorporated city, located near the small town of Fairfield, where the Maharishi had already established a university.

Maharishi International University had originally been located in Santa Barbara, California, but in 1971, in order to expand, the university's administrators chose to buy the campus of the former Parsons College in Fairfield, Iowa, and to relocate the university and a small related elementary school to the new site. Rapid growth of both schools followed immediately, as many of the Maharishi's followers moved to the new location so that their children could attend the school and they could participate in the growth of a new spiritual community.

By 1981 the school included grades K–twelve, graduating its first class of seven students in 1983. The spiritual community continued to grow quickly, especially after two large golden domes for meditation were completed in 1987.

In 2001, with the official state incorporation of Vedic City (population at the time: 136), the town became both a model and a focal point for the Maharishi's programs throughout the world. In November of 2001 the city council voted to rename the municipality Maharishi Vedic City in honor of its revered mentor.

From its inception, Maharishi Vedic City has embodied numerous elements of the Maharishi's plan. Each aspect addresses a particular fundamental element of people's lives.

Maharishi *Sthapatya Veda* design, according to the city's web site (maharishivediccity.net), is the science of building in harmony with natural law in order to create "health, happiness and good fortune." This architectural approach is built into each structure in the entire city. Every building faces to the east. Likewise, each edifice incorporates into its structure a special silent space at its center and includes golden ornamentation on its roof that is known as a *kalash*. Streets run north–south and east–west, and each small community is surrounded by a belt of evergreen trees. Beautiful parks, pavilions, gardens, lakes, and trails complement the architecture and landscaping of the buildings.

The vision for Vedic City includes plans for it to eventually meet all its utility needs from the sun and other renewable sources, according to the town's web site. Buildings are designed for energy efficiency, and they use natural building materials. Greywater waste will be recycled through use in gardens and greenhouses. Native grasses and ponds are used on the golf course and for retaining storm water to be reused in the environment.

Another part of the plan is Maharishi *Gandharva-Ved*, which involves the learning and playing of classical Vedic music. Taught in courses and played in homes, on radio stations, and in concerts worldwide, this peace–inspiring music produces a soothing influence on every individual it touches.

Maharishi *Ayur-Ved*, the holistic program of health care that was begun previously in Lancaster, Massachusetts, has been incorporated into the city's activities. The Raj Hotel and Resort, which has been ranked among the top ten spas in the country, offers Ayurvedic treatments that target specific diseases as well as programs that focus on the building of vibrant natural health.

Maharishi *Vedic Farming* brings many of the best practices of organic farming into harmony with the principles of natural law found in the Vedas. Since agriculture is considered one of the cornerstones of the city's economic development, the city has made plans for the gradual construction of 100 acres of greenhouses on already purchased land outside the town, in order for enough fresh, high–quality organic fruits and vegetables to be grown to supply the year–round needs not only of Vedic City but also of numerous other markets throughout the Midwest. Fresh produce is already offered in the university dining hall, in local food markets, and in various restaurants throughout the city.

The town's economic plan also calls for the development of new businesses within the city and the attraction of other commercial enterprises from around the U.S. A retirement community is also being planned, utilizing the positive elements already inherent in the environment: lack of crime, a wealth of educational programs, outstanding local produce, established natural health care, and numerous housing and recreation options that promote optimum well–being in both body and mind.

Education through the Maharishi's *Science of Creative Intelligence* remains a major focus in the community as both the Maharishi School of the Age of Enlightenment and the Maharishi Ideal Girls School continue to expand, and three universities—Maharishi University of Management (formerly Maharishi International University), Maharishi Open University (a global university accessible by satellite all over the world), and Maharishi Spiritual University of America (which offers special consciousness-based education for young women)—offer a wide range of courses on bachelor's, master's, and Ph.D. levels. In addition, the Brain Research Institute conducts scientific exploration into the enormous possibilities of the human mind. Also continuing to be built are local Maharishi Vedic Schools and TM Program Centers in major cities around the world, designed to disseminate the inner awareness and outer manifestation of the next level of human consciousness.

Administration of Vedic City is based on natural law and the application of Vedic principles. The government structure includes a mayor and a city council. Council minutes are available to all, and many of the issues brought before the council are submitted to the city's voters for decision.

In February 2002 the city council adopted Raam Mudra as Vedic City's official currency. According to the town's web site, this was planned as a means to "support economic development in the city" and to contribute to the growth of its businesses. Raam Mudra (similar to the innovative "Ithaca Hours" currency used in Ithaca, N.Y.) is exchangeable at the rate of one Raam for $10 in U.S. funds, and it is offered in one-, five-, and ten-Raam paper notes. Change of less than one Raam is given in U.S. dollars and cents.

Finally, Vedic City plans to take its special place in the accomplishment of world peace as part of what the Maharishi has called the Global Country of World Peace. The Vedic City web site states that this virtual Global Country is dedicated to creating world peace through the establishment of enough meditating *sidhas* (see chapter seventeen for an explanation of this level of consciousness) to create a strong "influence of coherence" for peace throughout the world. Vedic City plans to build up a cadre of 8,000 yogic flyers meditating in the city at all times in order to stabilize peace in America. At the same time, a peace-keeping group of 40,000 vedic pandits, meditating around the clock in India, will generate the same influence for the entire world. Peace-keeping groups of between 100 and 1,000 in each of the 3,000 largest cities of the world will lock in the peace influence at specific places around the globe.

It is an immense plan. Yet if it is successful, the world may very well see, as a result, the beginning of a totally new level of human consciousness and the advent of a true heaven on earth.

Part
Three

13

Aquativity, Sound Waves, Subtle Energies: Balancing the Body/Minds of Children

J ust at the time when children are being born with abilities that seem unusual to many people, so also a number of vibrational methods of healing have come more into common usage and greater public awareness during recent years. Perhaps this is because the children now incarnating have physical and emotional sensitivities that are better served by these more subtle modes of healing than by the coarser procedures of the past. Or perhaps our group awareness as a whole has been raised to the point where these methods have become more acceptable. Whatever the reason for greater acceptance, it does seem that these new healing modes are more in attunement with the vibrations of the children currently coming into incarnation.

One of the new healing methods is called

Aquativity. It involves subtle physical and mental movement within a water environment, stimulating the body's nerve centers while at the same time opening the psyche to healing and spiritual growth.

Another method is Sound Wave Energy. It introduces into the body, through sound frequencies, all of the elements found in nutritional foods. Each element within the physical body has a unique atomic weight, and the frequencies of the individual sounds used in this healing modality are keyed directly to the atomic weights of the various organic chemicals that make up a healthy body. Simply being in the same room while these sound CDs are playing allows the healthy vibrations to be absorbed. Going even further, other CDs in this series correlate to even more subtle energies, for healing and growth on the emotional and spiritual levels.

Finally, several vibrational tools that were suggested in the Edgar Cayce readings are gaining in popularity and usage. Among these are castor oil packs, the radial appliance (currently known as the Radiac), and the wet cell.

Castor oil, applied externally and kept warm, was suggested by Cayce in numerous physical readings. Castor oil apparently enters through the skin to stimulate the lymphatic system, drawing unwanted toxins out of the cells of the body and eliminating them through the lymph, liver, and intestines. The radial appliance (which looks like a large battery) was suggested by Cayce as a method for passing subtle electrical vibrations through the body, enhancing whatever positive vibrations were already there; for this reason, Cayce suggested that whatever was being read or pondered while an individual was using the radial appliance would actually become absorbed into the person's body as part of his or her personality and experience. Similarly, the wet cell also introduced vibrations into an individual body, but this modality was generally suggested when some nutrient was missing from or poorly absorbed by the body already; the wet cell introduced vibrationally into the body those elements that could not otherwise be brought into the physical system.

All of these healing modalities involve subtle forms of energy. Parents are encouraged to choose among them according to what seems right for their child. Different children will respond best to whatever forms most closely attune with their individual vibrational needs.

Aquativity

According to its founder, Priscilla Allen, Aquativity is an integrating experience of body, mind, and spirit in a water environment. Experienced as a series of meaningful events while floating in a body of water, Aquativity nourishes and stimulates the central nervous system and, in conjunction with this, releases emotions and opens the soul.

Allen emphasizes that Aquativity is not just the following of a certain procedure or the performing of a given set of exercises; it is much more than these. It is the harmonizing of an individual's heart and soul with the body and mind that makes it so powerful. It is the flowering of the beauty of spirit within the inner and outer human senses. Allen asserts that participants in Aquativity give expanded awareness to *themselves* through the subtle vibrational conductivity of water.

Priscilla Allen is a researcher and an educator who has discovered ways of bringing people back to the nursery that first nourished life on this planet—water—and of facilitating within it all the many unique benefits that this environment offers. Within her "water school," Priscilla gives students the tools for total personal awareness and freedom.

For more than fifty years, whenever Priscilla was in any body of water, she found that people who were experiencing difficulty seemed to gravitate toward her. Mothers brought their children with *spina bifida*, spinal cord injuries, arthritis, fibromyalgia, multiple sclerosis, muscular dystrophy, Attention Deficit Disorder (ADD), and Attention Deficit–Hyperactive Disorder (ADHD) to her. Other mothers whose infants were born with an immature central nervous system, cleft palate, or cerebral palsy also came. While floating in the water environment with Priscilla, many babies and children seemed to be helped in unexplained ways.

During the past fifteen years, Allen has devoted herself to evaluating—by using water as her laboratory—exactly what happens to people who are in the water with her. She has studied the effects of water on her own body and psyche as well. She is not a scientist nor a therapist and has never claimed to be one. What she does comes intuitively from her heart and soul, but she has spent years looking for answers as to what actually happens when she guides people to experience water in certain ways.

Like many people, Priscilla had felt an affinity with dolphins all her life, perhaps because she had spent so much of her life in the water. She had always wanted to swim with dolphins in the wild. Finally, once Priscilla began to try to understand why individuals were being helped so much physically and emotionally by being in the water with her, she had the opportunity to swim with dolphins.

After receiving a telepathic communication from the dolphins with whom she was swimming, Priscilla turned to them for information and answers to questions that she had been asking herself about her experiences with humans in the water. Receiving answers, she assumed they were coming from the dolphins, mainly because she had read reports of these animals communicating with human beings. Priscilla now knows that the guidance she received was from God, the highest source. In the beginning, however, because she thought that it was the dolphins who were teaching her, she was willing to listen. Later on she realized that it was not outlandish to believe that the guidance she had received was directly from God.

"God speaks to all of us in many and various ways," Priscilla says, smiling. "Only God truly knows the best way to touch our hearts."

Priscilla now takes her Aquativity classes and teacher-certification sessions to water spots around the globe. Wherever sensitive individuals are in need of water's conductivity as an added boost to their healing or personal growth, Priscilla will find a way to be there to help them.

Sound Wave Energy

Although Nicole LaVoie, as a young X-ray technician, was pregnant, she believed that the carefully placed shields protected her from any damaging rays. However, when her son, Robert, was born with multiple physical difficulties, she began to doubt the wisdom of that belief.

By the time Robert turned five, his body had stopped manufacturing key hormones, and he stopped growing. Hormone replacement therapy did little to help him. Nicole herself was having to deal with the devastating effects of osteoporosis. She left X–ray work and began to look for answers.

Frantic to help her son, Nicole pored over every kind of research she could find that might provide some hope for Robert. She studied Rife technology and homeopathy, she worked with crystals and became a Reiki master, and she delved into the workings of sacred geometry. Nicole found that Robert was unable to absorb certain nutrients. Eventually she discovered an amazing correlation between the atomic weights of these nutrients and the frequencies of particular musical notes in the lower octave ranges. Nicole found that when the corresponding sound frequencies were played over and over for a period of time in the same room with Robert, he gradually developed the ability to absorb those minerals.

Nicole was ecstatic! She realized that this was the key to many other people's difficulties, too. Nicole also began to realize that people's voice patterns gave clues to elements that were missing in their body systems. Traveling around in her soundmobile, Nicole made individualized audiotapes for people based on her evaluation of the frequencies present and absent in their speech. Eventually the demand was such that she needed to make more generalized tapes, and Sound Wave Energy was born.

Today Nicole is an internationally renowned lecturer and the author of *Return to Harmony: Creating Harmony and Balance Through the Frequencies of Sound*. Her Sound Wave Energy tapes and CDs are distributed globally, helping individuals around the world to rebalance their bodies and psyches and literally return to harmony.

As Sound Wave Energy expanded, Nicole began to have a growing vision of what she called an Awareness Center—a place where people could come to experience not only the balancing frequencies of sound but many other healing modalities as well. Today that vision is rapidly becoming a reality high in the mountains of Colorado. Nicole continues to expand her vision and her exceptionally important role in preparing individuals for the vibrations of the new consciousness in the earth.

Cayce Remedies: Castor Oil Pack, Radial Appliance, Wet Cell

Two principles of health and healing dominated the physical readings given by Edgar Cayce. One was that the health of the body, mind, and soul were so closely interrelated that it was rarely of value to treat any one of these aspects without also giving some attention to the state of the other two. The second premise was that, for every human ill, solutions were available from nature and the natural vibrations present in the earth. Together, these two assumptions formed the basis for the remedies suggested in the readings.

A third factor inherent in the Cayce readings was that, with few exceptions, they were given for individuals with different needs. This explains why there might be a slight variation in formula, product, manner of application, etc., even between readings on the same subject. Certain products and formulas, however, were recommended so repeatedly and emphatically that they have become almost specific for certain types of difficulties.

The recommendations from the Edgar Cayce readings that follow should not be viewed as do-it-yourself doctoring prescriptions. *Any of these suggestions in treatment of disease should be used under the supervision of a medical professional.*

Castor Oil Pack

The use of castor oil packs was advised in over 500 of the Cayce readings. They were recommended for poor eliminations, incoordination between nervous systems, epilepsy, various liver conditions, headaches, neuritis, arthritis, and toxemia. Individuals using the packs with children have reported that the packs have aided intestinal absorption of foods, helped balance energies, positively affected behavior, and improved general physical health. Research indicates that castor oil packs stimulate circulation in the lymphatic system for better elimination of toxins and residues. In some readings, Cayce suggested that parents combine the castor oil packs at bedtime with spinal massage, uplifting stories, and/or presleep suggestions. (See chapter sixteen for information on presleep suggestion.)

Following are suggestions for preparing and using a castor oil pack:

Materials:

Cotton or wool flannel cloth

Bottle of castor oil (preferably cold pressed)

Baking soda, water, and bowl or jar

Piece of plastic

Electric heating pad

Plastic baggie

Instructions for Use: Prepare a soft flannel cloth which when folded to two to four thicknesses, measures about ten inches in width and twelve to fourteen inches in length. This is the size needed for abdominal applications. Other areas may need a different size pack. Wool flannel is preferred, but cotton flannel is all right if there is an allergy to wool or wool is not available.

Carefully pour some castor oil onto the cloth. This can be done without soiling if a piece of plastic is placed underneath the cloth. Make sure the cloth is wet but not drippy with the oil.

Apply the wet cloth to the area which needs the treatment (usually on the abdomen, reaching from the liver or rib area on the right side of the body to the caecum or pelvic bone area). Place the piece of plastic over the flannel cloth, and put the heating pad on top of the plastic. Turn the heating pad to low heat.

Leave the pack in place for an hour if possible. This is a good time for inspirational reading, soft music or restful songs, prayer time, and/or loving presleep suggestions.

For children with sensitive skin, you may want to cleanse the abdomen afterward by adding 1 teaspoon of baking soda to 1 pint of warm water (or ½ tsp. of baking soda to 8 oz. of warm water). Use this solution to wipe over the area that was affected by the castor oil. Rinse with plain warm water.

Place the folded flannel cloth in an airtight plastic baggie for future use.

Frequency: Once a day for three to five days in a row, then skip the rest of the week, and repeat the packs the next week for the same number of days as before. This pattern may be continued for several weeks, or for several years!

Prayer: Some of the Cayce readings recommended that parents pray during the time the child was being ministered to. Various readings suggested that parents use their own words, with the essence being: *"The Father of light and mercy and truth, create in this body that as will bring the perfect coordination of the members of the body itself, that the soul may manifest in a perfect body."* (1314–2) Reading inspirational books is another possibility for spiritual uplift during the period of a child's castor oil pack.

Radial Appliance

The Radial Appliance, which Cayce often called the Radio–Active Appliance or the Impedance Device, was mentioned some 455 times in his readings. Despite the name, there is nothing truly radioactive about this device, at least not according to our modern understanding of that term. This healing tool looks like a large battery and produces a vibrational current that can affect in a very positive way every organ and tissue of the individuals who use it regularly as long as they maintain a positive mental and spiritual attitude during the period the appliance is being applied (usually by reading or hearing uplifting material during this time). It does not generate any measurable electrical energy of and by itself, but when used in conjunction with a physical human body, it has the ability to positively affect all the electrical energies of that particular body.

The Cayce readings recommended the use of the Radial Appliance to improve circulation and to normalize the functioning of the nervous system, thus aiding in the relaxation of the physical body. It was generally given more as a preventative than as a cure for serious physical problems, although in some cases the appliance was suggested as a help for one or more of the following: nervous tension, nerve incoordination, blood circulation, muscle coordination, insomnia, neurasthenia, debilitation, hypertension, certain abnormalities in children, deafness, obesity, and arthritis. Some parents have used it successfully—along with dietary modifications, castor oil packs, spinal massage, and presleep suggestions—with their children who have had difficulties related to behavior control and hyperactivity. Dr. Gladys McGarey in Scottsdale, Arizona, has been especially helpful with parents who wish to work with the Radial Device.

The Cayce readings often commented that the plain Radial Appli-

ance would be beneficial for almost anyone—enhancing personal balance and even physical longevity—so long as instructions for proper
usage were observed. "You can't use the Radio–Active Appliance . . . and
be a good hater," said Cayce in reading 1844–2. "For it will work as a
boomerang to the whole of the nervous system if used in conjunction
with such an attitude." However, Cayce suggested that this device would
give a wonderful opportunity for spiritual balance and for the perfec-
tion of coordination in physical, mental, and spiritual forces if used in
conjunction with "the body being kept in attunement . . . " (1800–5)

Unlike the Wet Cell Appliance, which can be used by multiple individuals, the Radial Appliance should be used by only one person exclu-
sively. However, if applied properly, the Radial Appliance should last a
lifetime, whether used once a day or once a year.

Wet Cell Appliance

The Wet Cell Appliance, like the Radial Appliance, is a battery. The
Wet Cell, however, produces a very small but measurable electric current that apparently stimulates the growth of nerve tissue and strength-
ens the connections between nerve tissues. The Wet Cell was referred to
in the Cayce readings about 975 times, each one for a very specific condition rather than for general use.

This device was suggested for a wide variety of physical and mental
disturbances, such as multiple sclerosis, insanity, arthritis, paralysis, re-
tarded mental development in children, Parkinson's disease, and deafness. Most often it seemed to be preferred in those cases that required
the rebuilding of tissue and the restoration of healthy function.

Cayce indicated that in using the Wet Cell, attachments were to be
made with lead wires to specific areas of the body, varying according to
the condition diagnosed. Specific mineral solutions were almost always
included in the circuit, to supply elements to the body vibrationally. In
many cases Cayce stated that this vibrational intake would be far more
beneficial than taking in the minerals through the digestive system. It is
generally recommended that the Wet Cell Appliance be used under the
supervision of a physician.

Each of these Cayce–recommended procedures and devices operates on a subtle vibrational basis that can be especially helpful to the currently incarnating children who are already highly responsive to vibratory rates. If offered by parents with the proper attitude and in an appropriate atmosphere, they hold enormous potential for helping to bring balance and optimum well–being to the bodies, minds, and spirits of our supersensitive Indigo, Psychic, and Crystal Children.

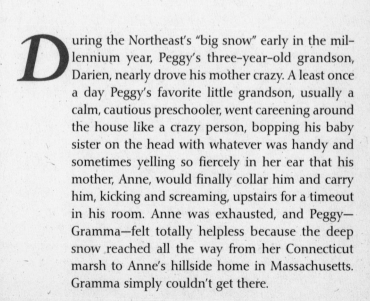

14

Intuitive Parenting

During the Northeast's "big snow" early in the millennium year, Peggy's three-year-old grandson, Darien, nearly drove his mother crazy. A least once a day Peggy's favorite little grandson, usually a calm, cautious preschooler, went careening around the house like a crazy person, bopping his baby sister on the head with whatever was handy and sometimes yelling so fiercely in her ear that his mother, Anne, would finally collar him and carry him, kicking and screaming, upstairs for a timeout in his room. Anne was exhausted, and Peggy—Gramma—felt totally helpless because the deep snow reached all the way from her Connecticut marsh to Anne's hillside home in Massachusetts. Gramma simply couldn't get there.

Peggy prayed a lot. She talked to Anne at least once a day on the phone, hoping to give her a chance, at the very least, to release some of her pent-up feelings. Then one morning Peggy came out of meditation simply knowing what needed to be done: she needed to look in the Cayce readings for what had been suggested to people like Anne for answering their deeply felt parenting needs. As Peggy searched the readings, she often laughed, partly because the solutions were so simple and partly because for years, as a volunteer in the A.R.E. Youth and Family Life Department, she had been telling A.R.E. parents to do every one of those things already! Physician, heal thyself!

Unfortunately many times the very things we find the most upsetting are the very things that a loving Creator has designed to get our attention so we can be helped the most. Concurrent with Darien's seeming change of personality was the winding down of Peggy's master's degree program at Atlantic University and the need for her to write a thesis or—as seemed more appropriate to her—design a community service project in lieu of a thesis. Suddenly the two problems came together in Peggy's awareness of a single solution. One morning she woke up just knowing that she could answer her heartfelt wish to help her daughter and grandson by designing a service project that would address their very needs. "Wow!" she said to God. "You are so good! Thank You!"

From then on for the next several weeks, information seemed to pour in from the universe. An unexpected telephone call came from Amy Kay, then-manager of the A.R.E. Youth and Family Life Department. Although Amy had phoned to ask about a parenting handbook that Peggy had helped compile in the early 1990s, somehow the subject of Peggy's possibly designing a parenting project through Atlantic University came up, and Amy bubbled over with enthusiasm at the prospect. She wanted Peggy to get started right away!

Cleaning off her desk to start typing on the project, Peggy found a previous issue of *Venture Inward* magazine and Dr. Christiane Northrup's newsletter *Health Wisdom for Today's Woman*, both of which included articles about using dreams to help a current situation. Her fingers seemed to fly on their own over the keys as Peggy downloaded and typed excerpts from the Cayce readings that she had already found. Materials she had gathered from the A.R.E. over a ten-year period suddenly seemed to pop out at her from every shelf and file drawer in her small study room: a booklet written by Charles Thomas Cayce about his own graduate-school research project using presleep suggestion with juvenile offenders; a research project that Peggy had helped parents work with in the early 1990s, one that included presleep suggestions and had been such a success; the parenting handbook that Amy had called about, with its suggestions about dreams and prayer and presleep suggestions; a former insert from the A.R.E. Membership Department, "Extracts from the Readings," that included the same information about answering "yes or no" questions in meditation that she had found directly from her own search of the Cayce readings; and several many-years-old invitations to participate in A.R.E. home-research projects that included specific instructions on how to go about working with such projects at home. Peggy was grateful for each and every one. They all seemed to confirm and expand what she had already found.

Then one morning she remembered another former A.R.E. home-research project—one she had participated in that had affected her profoundly. In an instant she knew that that deeply meaningful project needed to be the template for the project she was now working on. Peggy sensed that the awe and the high energy she had felt during that self-research needed to be poured into this new project. She spent several days eagerly looking through all the file drawers in her study room. She pulled every paper off every shelf. She even trudged down to the basement to look through the folders in several boxes of old papers there. But the material didn't seem to be anywhere. Finally wearing down a few nights later, Peggy began to feel so tired that she couldn't focus any more. It was then that she realized she hadn't prayed for higher help in the search. She slumped down on the daybed couch in her study, centered herself as best she could, and prayed a deep and intense prayer. She asked God to please, please help, saying that if it were God's will for her to initiate this project and to find and use this former research project as a format for the new one, could she please have some clues along the way. She said she would look one more time, and if she didn't find the old project, she would take that as a sign that she was supposed to design the project some other way. Then she sat quietly, allowing the peacefulness of God's presence to fill her soul.

Never in her life had Peggy experienced anything like the quietly amazing event that unfolded next. After her prayer, she stood up and walked slowly over to the main file cabinet, pulled open the top drawer and reached for the first file in the nearest batch of folders. As she picked up the file and held it up to the light, she could see that the penciled title said "Synchronicity and Guidance"—the very file she had been look-ing for for days! Clutching the purple folder like a precious treasure, she sank back down onto the daybed, and with full eyes and a grateful heart she opened it up. Yes, there were the write-ups of dreams about cousins she hadn't seen for years. And there was the spontaneous list of over thirty names and birth dates in specific relationships within her own family that exactly matched ones in the extended family of Edgar, Hugh Lynn, and Gertrude Cayce and also quite a few in Gladys Davis's family—parents, grandparents, in-laws, siblings, aunts, uncles, cousins, children, and grandchildren. Peggy suddenly had an inner image of the A.R.E. as her own "extended family." She sensed that the new project had the potential of helping those of her "family" who needed special help just now, with their children who would one day as adults bring in a whole new level of human consciousness. Peggy didn't know what to think. But she knew what she *felt*. It seemed to her that she was being told that God *did* want her to do this project!

Even before beginning to type up the new project formally into a specific format, Peggy had already begun to use the material from the Cayce readings to help her daughter find answers to young Darien's difficulties. Using presleep suggestion for herself each night as she fell asleep, Peggy came up with a number of ideas. Each one became the focus of a telephone discussion with Anne the next day, to see whether the information was something that Anne would feel comfortable using with Darien. Peggy was amazed at how easily the wordings for her own presleep suggestion flowed, until she remembered that she had spent over two years helping other A.R.E. parents make up presleep scripts to read to their children during a previous Child Behavior Research Project. After the first week, Darien seemed to be having fewer manic episodes.

Next Peggy experimented with taking a "yes or no" question into meditation. It was here that she realized that she hadn't actually honed a specific question for the whole problem, so she had to stop and do that first. Now Peggy knew why the presleep suggestion, while it had helped, hadn't totally solved the difficulty—she hadn't pinpointed the question she wanted answered! She felt a little silly. After all, that was the first thing she had always asked parents to do in the previous research project—to figure out *exactly* what they wanted for their child. Well, she was learning.

The "yes or no" in meditation produced some major breakthrough ideas, which Anne happily implemented and Peggy enjoyed hearing about over the phone. One was teaching Darien some rudimentary self-observation and self-control by talking frequently with him during his calm periods about expectations and consequences, as well as quietly but firmly reminding him of these at the start of any of his wild moods. Another "win" that came out of this meditation method was Anne's understanding that she should include some specific one-on-one time with her son each day, time that she now realized had been diminishing since her baby daughter's birth. Darien had apparently already been feeling the effects of having to share his world with a new baby sister, and now he was sensing it even more since the snow kept his entire family snowbound. Without frequent opportunities to go out to nursery school, play with nearby friends, or spend the usual quality time with Gramma, Darien was more and more often angry at baby Michelle. Now *everyone* was learning!

As Peggy started to formalize these first two procedures into a workbook format for other families, she began to use the third method herself: seeding and remembering dreams. This one, too, was especially easy for her, since she'd been seeding dreams off and on since her first remembered dream at age four. It had started one night when her mother ended the reading of a chapter in *The Wonderful Wizard of Oz* with Dorothy and her Oz friends stopped short by a seemingly endless wall that they couldn't get over. Peggy remembered being *really* worried about Dorothy and her friends, and she'd wanted to know how they would solve their problem so that they could continue on their way to find Glinda the Good.

That night four-year-old Peggy dreamed all about what happened next to Dorothy. In the morning, at breakfast, when Peggy eagerly told her mother about what the Oz friends did next, the shocked reply was, "Shame, Peggy! Did you get your sister to read the next chapter to you?" Peggy never told about her dreams again. But after that, whenever Peggy could actually remember to *want* answers strongly enough, she found that she could seed a dream any time she wanted to.

Perhaps Peggy had gotten too cocky about her ability to produce dreams. At any rate, she batted zero when she now tried to seed dreams that would hold answers for Darien and Anne. In fact, Peggy remembered no dreams the entire week! Eventually she just laughed at herself and went on to the next method.

The final suggestion Peggy had found in the Cayce readings was that of deep, sincere prayer, combining an individual's prayers with the power of a group praying for that person at the same time. Again Peggy knew from personal experience the incredible power of sincere group prayer. When her daughter's doctor had become concerned, during Anne's recent pregnancy, about a possible rubella infection that Darien's daycare provider had warned about, Peggy had actually *felt* the prayers from her A.R.E. Search for God study group as well as from the regional Power of Prayer (POP) team and the A.R.E. Glad Helpers Prayer Group—and Michelle was born tiny but perfectly healthy (and smiling since birth!). So Peggy asked her study group to pray again—this time for Anne, Darien, and herself—each day for a week. Again she basked in the warmth of that loving energy, and she sensed that Darien felt it, too. Anne reported that he was just about back to his old calm self.

Then the snow began to melt, Peggy could get back up to Massachusetts for her weekly visits, and life was pretty much back to normal again. But something had changed. Anne and Peggy continued to use some of the insights from those snowbound weeks as well as to try out some new possibilities that came up afterward. Perhaps they had become more sensitized to their intuition. At any rate, they enjoyed exploring new vistas, like attending a family gym period each week and sharing inspirational stories with the children and each other. Peggy felt closer to both Anne and Darien through the experience.

Because of her own encounters with seeking answers through inner guidance, Peggy was not surprised to find that other families working with the formalized pilot project (soon titled the Intuitive Parenting

Project) also had wonderful breakthroughs along with their highs and lows. The weeks of deep snow had given Peggy the time to write up the project, and eventually she met with Amy Kay in Virginia Beach, where Amy's assistant Rachel Greenberg miraculously turned the manuscript into a work of art with her computer, and the printing department presented Peggy with professionally bound, real-life workbooks! Amy advertised the project in *Venture Inward* magazine for interested parents, and one by one the phone calls began to come in.

A few parents at a time worked hard on their questions and answers. By the time they were done with the project, Peggy felt as though they were genuinely her "family" as well as her friends. Almost all the parents who participated in the pilot project felt that the time spent strongly focusing on answering their questions helped them gain insights and find synchronistic confirmations along the way. Just as Peggy had found in using the Cayce methods herself, some parents had great success with certain procedures and received no insights at all with others. But the most interesting part of that information was that not one of the methods was without at least one family who considered that procedure the best of all!

One father reported that it was the presleep suggestion that provided him with the most helpful of all the intuitive information he received during the project. In his evaluation of the program, he indicated that he was given synchronistically during that week both warnings about his own need for healing old wounds (which he immediately acted on) and positive encouragement for helping his son overcome similar difficulties. "This project was a great blessing to me," he wrote, saying that it also "arrived in a very timely manner for the difficulty it addressed." Additionally, he said that his son, too, "responded very well to presleep suggestion and, ironically enough, I think I will use this same tool the most in my own life questions."

A mother, who indicated that using the "yes or no" question in meditation was one of the best tools for her and her son, found that, when she asked, the answer was that it was meditation itself that would help her son the most. She said that her son was not a morning person and that he often met her requests dealing with routine a.m. activities with "NO!" But when she would mention that it was time for the meditation they had begun doing daily before school (and he often reminded *her* that it was time for it), he would run to his bedroom ready for the session, even saying, "Oh good! I love this." She also indicated that "he told me after our first meditation that he heard God tell him he would accomplish his life's mission." After another meditation, she said, "He saw a path with lots of side paths branching off but was told none of the side paths were for him and he should stay on the main path." Needless to say, she was very happy to have her son share with her a love of meditation.

Another mother reported that she didn't have any inner response at all to the "yes or no" question asked in meditation. However, immediately *after* the meditation she heard an inner voice that gave her a lot of wonderful information in response to her original question, including the understanding that music, particularly Celtic and/or New Age music but also any "soothing, happy music," would be very helpful for her son. Just after this experience, her son called her from the town where he was visiting to tell her that he had just bought a CD of New Age Celtic music that was so "soothing and happy" (using the very words that she had heard following meditation!).

A father reported that the days on which he used "yes and no" questions in meditation made up the period during the entire project when "I was best able to consolidate the guidance I received into actions to take. The questions which came to me each day during this week really guided me through a process." He noted that this method was one that he was especially attracted to, but that it was the finding of the questions themselves that had held the most significance for him, since he had few if any insights from the actual meditation–answering process.

One mother said that while looking for guidance through dreams, she didn't have any luck actually incubating a dream, but on one of the nights when she didn't happen to ask, she had a very, very significant one. All the elements in the dream seemed either actually or symbolically related to her young teenaged son's difficulties. Another unsolicited dream encouraged her that her son was "doing great" and that she needed to keep on doing what she was doing, thinking continuously of him as being totally well.

A father called Peggy excitedly one week to say that he had "*wonderful* news" about how powerfully prayer works. "Things have been incredibly beautiful, loving, great!" he said. He indicated that he had actually *felt* the love from all the people praying for him (the POP team). He told Peggy that his son had just been accepted at a Waldorf school and that he, the father, had participated in an amazing circle of love that weekend in which he was hugged by each person and told how wonderful he was—imbuing him for the first time in his life with the sense that he was indeed both loved and lovable. He had basked in that love all week and planned to continue to attend the circle meetings. He had also been drawn to read a book that he said "touched me deeply in my soul." He found that one of the basic premises of the book (by Jewish sages) was true in his own life—that when one's own thinking and actions have been strongly affected, it carries over to others, too. He already saw that the changes in himself had begun making a difference in his son's behavior.

Another father indicated that the answers he received during the prayer week were similar to those given to him during the period of presleep suggestion. He said that dreams he had during this time strongly reinforced the information he had received synchronistically and intuitively while using the presleep method.

A mother reported that positive changes occurred spontaneously in her *other* children while she was working on the project, even though she was concentrating on only one child. One mother also found that she had to avoid a question that would *make* her child "be good"—i.e., she had to reword her question so that it was not, as another mother said about her own realization, "such a little question." The former mother had to change her question to something broader and more positive when her son began to come down with a cold as she concentrated on wanting him to be more obedient and courteous. She admitted that he was a very sensitive child, but she was taken aback that the intense concentration of her question on him would have such a strong effect on his physical body!

Overall Peggy found that the parents who participated in the Intuitive Parenting pilot project were happy with the results and were glad that they had been involved in it. She felt that way herself.

The next winter when deep snow covered the ground again and

Peggy couldn't get to Massachusetts for her usual weekly visit, she asked Anne how Darien was doing.

"Fine," said Anne, "except when his blood sugar is low or he needs to run off some energy. The good part is that I know now how to head off the symptoms, so I just feed him or make up a race course!"

Most parents who use their intuition while asking questions that may genuinely help their children find that the answers really do come—with a bit of help from higher sources!

(Intuitive Parenting Project workbooks are available from A Place of Light. Write to friendsofapol@myexcel.com)

15

Edgar Cayce on Parenting for the New Consciousness

*E*dgar Cayce's psychic readings stated over and over that we are all spiritual beings seeking reconnection or reunion with God. If we as an entire humanity wish to move closer in our relationship to the Creative Forces, we need to take a deeper look at what specific attitudes and actions will both allow and facilitate our children's development within this new consciousness.

The Cayce readings suggested that the innate soul impulse to reunite with God can be fostered by all participants in a child's environment. Cayce also gave some specific recommendations for this guidance.

According to the readings, children are mature souls in immature bodies. The very possibility that a child, as a reincarnating soul, has already had a great deal of experience in the earth can help parents to view him or her in a different light and help parents to think more about the potential for spiritual growth within each child.

The readings also made it clear that the type and quality of the home environment and the guidance a child experienced in the first twelve to fourteen years of his or her life (and especially during the first seven-year cycle, from birth to age seven) were of primary importance to the development of the soul in that entire lifetime.

A study of the Cayce readings on child guidance quickly reveals a number of basic principles that serve as the basis for all the specific techniques that were given; principles such as setting ideals and teaching by example. As we dig a bit deeper, it is soon clear that parents are being urged and inspired to be, say, and do one primary thing: *LOVE*. Or, put another way, to strive to see the best in every way in themselves and in others. Such an attitude teaches the children in one's care far more than any words or techniques.

Cayce spoke of the interconnectedness of body, mind, and spirit. The body, he said, was the temple, and, if treated with care, would aid and cleanse the mind and spirit. The mind was seen as the builder, where bodily healing and change originated. And the spirit was the life, infusing mind and body with transforming grace and beauty. This essential oneness, which pervaded the entire Cayce readings, is of utmost importance.

The spiritual dimension was, for Cayce, the foundation upon which everything else rested. The Cayce readings urged that children be exposed to people, surroundings, and experiences that were inspirational and uplifting, demonstrating the fruits of the spirit in action. The readings also encouraged a sense of mystery and wonder, spoke of the value of nature and its inherent spiritual content, and made suggestions for the nourishment and development of a healthy body, imagination, and will. Most of all Cayce advocated a close personal attunement with the Creative Forces (God) through daily meditation, prayer, and attention to dreams.

Cayce saw the home as having the potential of being the most powerful influence possible in the development of any soul in a lifetime. Cayce indicated that the people, the physical environment, and the family lifestyle all had an exceptionally strong impact on the soul of the child during the first twelve to fourteen years, carrying over into adulthood as major patterns. For parents and prospective parents, this meant that the work of creating a home was of utmost importance. How the parents lived their own lives and what they brought into the home (physically, mentally, and spiritually) could affect children more than anything else in their lives!

The spiritual ideals, attitudes, thoughts, actions, and responses of all parents have enormous cumulative impact on what their children sense, desire, and ultimately become. Of course, children do bring much with them from their personalities in past lives. Of course, no parents themselves are absolutely perfect! But there is much to be gained by parents' looking closely at themselves and at the images that they are projecting to their children. In this way they can prepare themselves to be the examples they knowingly want to be. For parents, the setting of personal spiritual ideals, taking time daily for meditation, regular writing in a personal journal or dream log, and spending time each week with spiritually oriented friends (perhaps in a formal or informal study group) can be well worth the time used.

The Cayce readings indicated that each soul actively chose the parents through whom he or she incarnated and the environment into which he or she manifested, in order to meet the conditions and purposes desired for a particular lifetime. Cayce told parents that the setting and atmosphere of the home—physical, psychological, and spiritual—were literally created from all who participated in it.

Because the home constantly provides images to all who live in it and draw from it, parents need to consciously create an ideal to focus their energies on. If they fail to do this, then whatever forces are present daily (such as selfishness, anger, TV images, peer pressure, etc.) will be the guiding elements in the life of the child and the family. However, if children are constantly surrounded by the experience, consciousness, and symbols of their spiritual Source, then that will become the directing force in their lives.

Taking the time to choose a family ideal for the home (e.g., "a place where one feels loved") can be a very worthwhile activity. Finding informal routines or occasions that embody this ideal can be especially helpful—such as a special greeting in the morning or at bedtime, little affirming messages on a table by the door, special routines at mealtime or bedtime, or special celebrations related to the seasons or to family remembrances. Taking time occasionally to talk with children about what they like about their home can further result in better family communication, understanding, and sharing.

Parents, especially, need to remember the value of balance in all things. Balance was one of the keynotes of the Cayce readings—enough of each part of life but not too much. Suggestions for balance included finding equivalent time for physical, mental, and spiritual activities, time alone and time with others, regular routines but not forced rituals, time for work and time for play. The readings especially emphasized the finding of natural rhythms. In the home, all of these elements are constantly in motion, and it is often the awareness of the parents that brings about the balance, as well as the parents' creativity that restores balance when it has been upset. It behooves parents to do a family check periodically to see that a balanced lifestyle is being maintained!

Another primary focus of the Cayce readings was on selfless doing for others—on living the Golden Rule. This very giving was viewed as a spiritual act—that by constantly doing small kindnesses, a child became more conscious of the positive attributes of giving to others, and more attuned to the spiritual principle of love behind the rule. One of Cayce's suggestions for helping children become aware of kindness was in telling and reading stories that nurtured compassion for others' hopes and feelings. Another suggestion was to actually do kind deeds for others (whether alone, as a family, or as part of a larger organization)—through words, thoughtful deeds, small tokens of caring, or other acts of kindness.

Since the spiritual dimension was of such primary importance in all the Cayce readings, it is not surprising that there were frequent suggestions made to individuals that they needed to be more in touch with or in tune with their spiritual Source. Such contact was shown to bring a greater sense of peace, a growing awareness of the Creative Forces, and a gradual awakening of the soul to a higher consciousness. If we are to nurture the next generation of children into a truly new consciousness, the spiritual aspect of family life becomes especially important.

According to the Cayce readings, a close association with nature in addition to attunement to the natural world allows its beauty—and the loving vibrations of its Creator—to enter the soul. In one reading, Cayce said, "he who understands nature walks close with God." (1904-2) This avenue was particularly recommended for children.

As parents, you can use whatever natural settings and opportunities are around you, taking time with your children to silently feel the spiritual manifestations in nature. As you do this over time, you gradually develop a great attunement to and appreciation for the God force that is within both nature and the self.

For many children, being attuned to nature can be a spiritually moving experience. Because these feelings can run deep, it may be difficult for a child to articulate them. As a parent, you can be sensitive to the mood of the moment. Encourage your child to express his or her feelings while being careful not to force that experience; rather, look for small gradual behavioral changes or verbal indications that an inner awareness is taking place. Take walks in various natural environments. Experience manifestations of nature in seasonal weather conditions: rain, snow, fog, wind. Watch a sunrise or sunset together; observe clouds, stars, trees. Listen for the sounds of nature. Plant a garden together and give away items from its bounty. All of these can tap deeply into a child's sense of God.

The Cayce readings also strongly encouraged prayer and meditation as fundamental tools for soul growth and development. Cayce suggested that prayer be thought of as talking to God, and meditation as listening to God speaking.

For children younger than twelve or thirteen years, the readings suggested that parents help *prepare* each child for making prayer and meditation important parts of their lives. Many young children will know instinctively how to pray and/or meditate; others will prefer to observe their parents. Many times the readings indicated that a parent's own prayers and meditations were the most important factors in this process. Praying for each child daily was suggested. Also, parents' awareness of meditation and prayer in their own lives would serve as a model that their children could emulate.

One parent told the story that he, as a very young child, found his father sitting quietly in the dark one morning, so he simply seated himself beside his daddy's leg and closed his eyes, too. Seeing a brilliant light behind his closed eyelids, he immediately opened his eyes to see where the light had come from. After opening and closing his eyes several times, he realized that the light was only on the "inside"—the "outside" was still quite dark. Later, he asked his dad about the light inside, and his father explained that he had seen the "light of the Christ" from his father's meditation!

One other emphasis in the Cayce readings—one that was almost always included when questions on prayer and meditation were asked—was on the family's overall spiritual life. The readings encouraged parents to give their children a love of spiritual things. This should be offered but not forced—through telling or reading well-loved stories, having informal conversations with or about God, giving affirmations during massage or other therapeutic procedures, and/or making presleep suggestions at bedtime. Always emphasizing the spiritual dimension of life, the readings encouraged seeing God in *all* of one's life.

Many of Edgar Cayce's readings for children advised working with their dreams. The readings viewed dreams as a natural experience, a gift of God for understanding the self, finding answers, discovering one's purpose in life, and, most important of all, awakening the spiritual consciousness. Parents were advised to help their children have a more meaningful dream life by simply encouraging them to share their dreams and by listening to their dream messages without judgment. Over time, such sharing could help children to gain special appreciation for these messages of the soul and to develop an understanding of dreams as a creative expression of the inner self. Gradually this can also lead to a deeper spiritual awareness of the God Force within. Having a special morning time for remembering and telling dreams, keeping a family dreambook, and/or following through on dreams in a physical way (e.g., helping a friend or planting a garden, if this was what was dreamed about) can help give a child a deeper awareness of the dream and its meaning, and can bring the reality of the dream symbols further into the waking experience of the self.

Over and over the Cayce readings emphasized that will is one of the primary God-given attributes of the soul. Cayce viewed the will as the inner power that allowed self–determination, self–control, and personal decisions. Through the will, the soul could use or abuse the Creative Force within. The Cayce readings were emphatic that during the formative years (the first twelve to fourteen years), parents must carefully and sensitively guide the child's will until he or she could use it appropriately to guide the self. The challenge for parents was to find creative ways to reach their child's inner self, enlist the self's choice to work with its highest purpose, and guide the child to choose, focus, and act on that ideal.

In any child the will manifests to a greater or lesser degree. For a child whose will was especially strong, the Cayce readings encouraged giving the child choices, within limits, to allow him or her to grow by positive, helpful use of the strong desires, hopes, and emotions that were already part of the self. For those whose wills were weak or broken, Cayce suggested encouragement to develop a stronger desire or determination gradually, through purposeful activity directed toward a goal in which the child was particularly interested. Cayce encouraged the use of stories of children and heroes who used their desires in positive ways, and the offering of choices or alternatives toward a purposeful goal. Most of all, parents were encouraged to be positive, patient, and gently firm.

Suggestions in the Cayce readings for guiding the will were for the most part given for specific children and, therefore, as in all the readings for individuals, they spoke to the particular needs of each person. However, Cayce researcher Carolyn Gelone in her book *Teaching for Wholeness* has categorized a number of types of children by temperament and personality, along with general directions from their individual readings that would suggest methods for training the will in that type of child. Some examples of Cayce's suggestions to parents were:

Argumentative child: Always give reasons, positively but firmly stated (1208–1)

Critical child: Direct the critical manner in constructive ways (1700–1)

Easily discouraged child: Help to set goals with a meaningful purpose (2572–1)

Emotionally harsh child: Guide in demonstrations of softer nature; reach with music (1227-1)

Fearful child: Be patient; never scold; love gently (3162-1)

Fearless child: Use reason, persuasion, and firmness to guide actions (3162-1)

Free-thinking child: Train to make beliefs practical in application (857-1)

Leader: Guide the thinking to include purposeful actions, not just self-glory (1332-1)

Quick-learning child: Train to watch for details, use reasoning (2308-1); balance the mental activities with physical activities (4084-1)

Strong-willed child: Train to act for constructive purposes; train by love and reason, not by driving him (1417-1)

The Cayce readings indicated that strong-willed children in particular needed to learn to discipline their wills under the tutelage of loving, firm, creative parents. The soul at birth was shown to already have a pattern of using its will, and parents were told they would do well not to take away from what had already been built within the soul, but to add to it positively by observing the individual, analyzing the child's strengths and manners of expression, raising the child's awareness of his or her actions, and finding ways to guide the child into making more and more positive choices in the self for purposeful, useful expressions and deeds. Cayce indicated that genuinely listening to the child and using reason, purposeful explanation, and constructive complimenting was the best avenue for helping children learn to use their strong wills in positive ways.

Over and over, the Cayce readings emphasized that a soul's first responsibility was to know itself in relation to God. If the will was directed consistently to the spiritual dimension, through an ideal that embodied the soul's highest purpose, then great soul growth could take place. The Cayce readings constantly held up before parents the necessity of making sure that the will was directed to the highest purpose.

Presleep suggestion was one method mentioned in the Cayce readings as an extremely helpful tool for parents to use to help their children develop constructive behavior patterns, change disruptive behaviors, learn more easily, and express their creativity more fully. The repetition of positive statements to the child as he or she went to sleep, said Cayce, instilled in the subconscious mind a suggestion which then became the experience of the child when awake. By using presleep suggestions, parents were encouraged to call upon the Divine within the child—that which was already whole and perfect—to become manifest in body and mind and to bring about positive, lasting change. In this way parents were given the option of working with the child's soul to create solutions through the subconscious instead of locking horns in a battle of wills on the conscious level.

Through presleep suggestion, parents would be able to work with the child's subconscious mind to help address any area of concern in the child's life—behaviors (such as bed-wetting or inappropriate actions during anger), emotions that might be hindering positive experiences (fear of visiting the dentist, school anxiety, or nervousness in a new situation), or even actually straightening teeth! Similarly, presleep suggestions were offered as helpful for developing greater spiritual or mental awareness, or creating a healthy physical body.

Parents were asked to put themselves into a prayerful state of mind, be specific about what changes they asked for their child, write out positive statements about the changed behavior and the child's feelings about it (as though they were already true), and include further statements about the child's being loved and affirmed. The parents would then read the statements over and over to the child each night for five to ten minutes as the child moved into sleep, fully relaxed but not yet in deep slumber. This period, according to the Cayce readings, was a time during which the "soul mind" could be impressed by suggestions that would result in positive changes within the waking mind and body.

As for the waking mind, the Cayce readings emphasized the importance of developing what was already there in each child's personality, guiding it in conjunction with the child's will for spiritual purposes. A child's creative imagination, encouraged, trained, and guided toward spiritual ends, would be able to combine with his or her natural desires to create and accomplish any goal.

The Cayce readings' emphasis on the development of strong, directed imaginative forces in children were part of a general encouragement to develop all that was constructive and creative in the child's mind. By guiding children to use their imaginations, parents were also encouraged to help them toward a closer relationship to the Creative Forces within and allow greater soul development. Over and over Cayce urged parents to guide the development of their children's imaginative mental forces in preference to materially oriented mental abilities.

Cayce described learning, understanding, and all education as "unfoldment." His readings suggested that the goal must be to reach and engage the whole child—body, mind, and spirit—and they indicated ways to engage the inner child as well as the mind in any learning activity. Parents were encouraged to follow their child's natural interests in order to arouse desire and will—to pique the curiosity, encourage questions, offer varied activities, give useful applications, and guide the child into seeing the oneness of everything in the Creative Forces. The use of desire, imagination, and practical application in *anything* one wanted to learn was foremost in Cayce's approach to education.

Besides offering suggestions for the soul and the mental forces, Cayce also gave information for nurturing the physical body. The Cayce readings emphasized that the physical body was the house of the soul, a temple of God. As such, said Cayce, it should be treated with great care and respect. Caring for the body included making sure that it received a balanced diet that emphasized foods with an alkalinizing effect on the body, sufficient exercise and rest, and a positive attitude. Although many of the Cayce readings were given for sick children who needed to heal, the readings also encouraged *preventive* measures so that the mental and spiritual forces in the child would have an optimum physical channel through which to manifest.

Dietary information given through Edgar Cayce was very much in keeping with today's best nutritional guidelines for disease prevention. Although most of the Cayce readings were specifically tailored to the needs of the individuals for whom they were given, certain suggestions recurred often enough to become noticeable patterns. These included a basic diet emphasis on foods that had an alkalinizing effect on the body, some general suggestions for daily menus, and the advice to avoid certain food combinations.

The general diet guidelines recommended in the Cayce readings were:
1. Plenty of fresh vegetables and fruits. These should be in season and

locally grown, if possible. Vegetables should be fresh or lightly steamed. Fresh juices were recommended. The readings suggested that 80% of a diet (four out of every five foods) should be alkaline-producing foods, of which vegetables and fruits were given as the major source. Almonds were also listed as alkaline-producing, while dairy products were neutral; grains, meats, vegetable protein foods, most nuts, and fats were listed as acid-producing foods.

2. Whole grain breads and cereals—including 100% whole wheat, rye, oat, and corn breads, plus grains, cereals, and pasta.

3. Nonfat or low fat dairy products—milk, buttermilk, cottage cheese, and yogurt; also, low fat cheeses, such as mozzarella and ricotta.

4. Fish, fowl, and lamb, and vegetable protein foods. Fish and shellfish, fowl (such as chicken, turkey, duck, goose), and lamb should be baked, broiled, or poached.

5. Nuts and seeds, especially almonds.

6. Six to eight glasses of plain water daily. Also herb teas and fresh juices. (Smaller amounts of water for young children.)

7. Only limited amounts of:
   - Oils and butter
   - Eggs
   - Honey
   - Cheese (those high in fat)
   - Wine
   - Desserts

8. Foods to avoid:
   - Fried foods
   - Refined foods (made with white flour or sugar)
   - Carbonated beverages
   - Beef (except for once a week or so)
   - Pork (except for occasional crisp bacon)
   - Alcohol (except for occasional red wine)

The Cayce readings also indicated that it was the alkaline or acid reaction of certain food *combinations* that was disturbing to most people's digestion. In some cases, the readings gave an explanation of exactly what it was that was disturbing about a given food combination, though in other cases they did not. The following food combinations were suggested in the readings to be avoided by most people:

1. **Citrus and milk, or citrus with cereal**. Citrus fruits are high-acid fruits, which cause milk to curdle and disturb the digestion when eaten with cereals. Whole wheat bread does not give this reaction, according to one reading, perhaps because the yeasting process alters the structure of the grain in some significant way. So much for cereal with milk and a glass of orange juice for breakfast! A better plan would be to eat a whole-grained cereal with milk at breakfast and have orange slices as a mid-morning snack several hours afterward, or whole wheat toast with orange juice alone.

2. **Raw apples with other foods.** It seems that the readings saw apples as a high-fiber internal cleanser. A three-day all-raw-apple diet was mentioned frequently as a cleansing regimen. Perhaps Cayce's reason for suggesting that people not eat apples with other foods was that they may bind nutrients from other foods during the digestive process. Apples do make a wonderful snack if eaten alone—they provide dietary fiber and do a reasonable job of cleaning the teeth as well. Cooked apples, in the form of baked apples or applesauce, can apparently be eaten at a meal with other foods, probably because the cell walls of the apples break down during the cooking process and are no longer able to bind nutrients effectively.

3. **Sugars and starches together.** These include fruit pies, cakes, cookies, and many other desserts. These foods are said to produce "an unbalancing in the alkalinity of the system" (340-32), because they are so acid-reacting in the body (and therefore make one more prone to colds). Instead, fresh fruit, fruit salads, baked apples, custards, sorbets, ice cream, yogurt, and other creative desserts that avoid the combination of sweet fruits or sugar with starches were recommended in the readings.

4. **Meats and starches together.** The Cayce readings explained that proteins and starches each required different digestive processes and that the combination of these two generally made for "disturbance with most physical bodies." (416-9) Too bad for the American hamburger! A better combination would be meat with vegetables, or

starch with vegetables. A meal should likewise not be made up of several starches (such as corn, potatoes, rice, or pasta) because nutritious nonstarchy vegetables would tend to be displaced in such a meal.

What about *helpful* food combinations? The readings suggested that citrus fruits or juices combined with other citrus fruits or juices was a beneficial combination (e.g., four parts orange or grapefruit juice mixed with one part lemon or lime juice, or all-citrus fruit salads). A good way to increase daily intake of vitamin, mineral, and fiber-rich alkaline-reacting vegetables would be to have one meal each day that contained a lot of fresh, raw vegetables together, such as a large salad. The readings suggested having three vegetables that grew above the ground to every one that grew below. Also, mixing gelatin with raw vegetables was said to enhance the assimilation of the nutrients in the vegetables.

Most of all, parents should teach themselves and their children to pay attention to signals from their own bodies, to find out what foods and food combinations work best for their individual systems.

Some suggestions for optimizing children's nutrition: Involve children in growing and cooking food, making it a fun time together. Let the children help with grocery shopping, allowing them to choose produce especially. Try out locally grown and organic foods. Keep food portions at meals small enough to be eaten easily. Make meals peaceful sharing times. Encourage relaxation just before eating, and serve each meal with Vitamin L: Love!

16

Edgar Cayce on Guiding Psychic Children

Reading 5752–1 was one that Edgar Cayce gave for himself as an adult to help him understand the nature of psychic ability. In this reading, psychic ability was defined as a manifestation of the soul forces working through the senses of the physical body. According to Edgar Cayce, this ability was inherent in *every* individual but it often lay dormant.

According to the Cayce readings, an individual's growth in, and awareness of, his or her own intuition depended to a great extent on whether or not these natural experiences were ignored, scolded, or allowed to be awakened. Psychic or soul energy, said Cayce, was helped or hindered by both the individual and the environment in which people found themselves. Cayce indicated that psychic energy usually manifested through whatever physical senses had been nurtured, encouraged, or honored. The ongoing development, however, was dependent upon how the awareness was used, as well as how individuals fed their bodies, their minds, and their souls with positive or negative subjects when thinking, reading, or acting.

One theme stood out in Cayce's advice for psychic children: that an enormous influence came from the parent(s) and the environment. Cayce suggested surrounding psychic children as much as possible with people who were open to intuitive experiences and yet who wouldn't overemphasize them. In addition, the readings advocated a family lifestyle that included a spiritual focus, a balanced approach to life, kind deeds done for other people, and opportunities for using creative energies through the arts.

As children reached age eleven or twelve and beyond, positive experiences with like-minded friends and accepting adults were suggested to help them set their own ideals, attune to their spiritual source, and understand themselves better. Although psychic ability would sometimes seem to fade during the teen years, sensitive adults could at least help their teenagers to understand themselves and to channel energies into creativity and the arts. At some later date these young individuals might choose to let their energies flow again into the psychic senses.

Cayce encouraged all parents to live in a balanced, natural way, and to create a home environment conducive to any child's normal development. As in many other readings for children, Edgar Cayce emphasized the need for *everyone* in the psychic child's environment (not just the parents and the child) to focus on creative and spiritual purposes. The Cayce readings encouraged parents to help their child find opportunities to participate in creative and imaginative activities (such as those related to art, music, movement, nature). Suggestions were made that a natural, balanced diet be part of the child's—and the family's—lifestyle. In fact, keeping a balance in *all* areas of life was especially encouraged for psychic children, because they sometimes had a tendency to go to extremes with their abilities.

In giving readings for psychic children, Cayce addressed many different types of intuitive abilities, often related to one of the outward physical senses, such as sight, hearing, or touch. For example, a child

SEEKING INFORMATION ON

**holistic health, spirituality, dreams,
intuition or ancient civilizations?
Call 1-800-723-1112, visit our Web site,
or mail in this postage-paid card for a FREE
catalog of books and membership information.**

Name: _____

Address: _____

City: _____

State/Province: _____

Postal/Zip Code: _____ Country: _____

PBIN

Association for Research and Enlightenment, Inc.
215 67th Street
Virginia Beach, VA 23451-2061
www.edgarcayce.org

For faster service, call 1-800-723-1112.

who was visually oriented might see images of past lives and also observe discarnate beings who had been known to him or her earlier in
the current life. In other cases, however, a child might begin by experiencing one type of psychic ability and later find it expanding into other
ways of perceiving. One scenario of this experience would be for a
child's psychic ability to come at first in dreams and later to manifest as
waking intuition or visions.

Oftentimes one particular sense was emphasized over others in one
particular reading, while another one might be mentioned as important
at a later time in the individual's life. Hearing might be emphasized in a
given experience, or seeing, or touch, or feeling, or intuition. Sometimes
children were shown to even have "normal" experiences that might not
ordinarily be recognized as "psychic"—such as flights of imagination or
memories of beautiful experiences.

One method suggested in the Cayce readings for parents to better
understand their children's psychic experiences was to observe whether
the events came from sensitivity to the *surrounding environment* or
whether they came from the child's *looking within*. Individual psychic
experiences could be triggered by either, but generally a parent could
find out through observation which pattern had already developed
within their child for receiving information.

Also, parents were asked to look at whether the experiences were
pleasant or frightening to the child. Cayce urged the parents of a very
fearful four-year-old girl (3162-1) to be especially patient and loving.
They were advised to tell her daily of Jesus' love of children, as well as
to use stories about peace and harmony. The parents needed to give
their daughter many gentle, happy images with which to feed her
dreams and visions. These parents were encouraged to help their child
see her intuition as a helpful influence rather than a disturbing one, so
that it could become a more positive influence in her life.

Often Cayce's counsel to young people with psychic abilities was to
strive for the highest purpose and not to get caught up in the fascination of the phenomenon itself. In one instance, Cayce urged a twelve-
year-old boy (1581-2) not to concentrate his energy on seeing
less-developed spirits in the "interbetween" but to concentrate
instead on a similar relationship with God, since this latter friendship

would offer him limitless growth.

Cayce often told parents to make certain that they showed their child how to focus on the positive, helpful aspects of the experiences. Some of the children who received readings were hypersensitive to their surroundings and, therefore, needed to be guided into choosing helpful friends and positive settings around whom and within which they could be safely open to psychic experiences. Cayce told many parents that they needed to teach their children how to make comparisons—helping their children learn to study and understand within themselves why some activities or experiences were better than others.

The foundations for all of Cayce's suggestions about psychic development were set out in readings 5752-1 and 5752-2, the original readings on psychic ability. Since psychic abilities were spiritual forces manifesting through an individual mind and physical body, said Cayce, then in order for the experiences to be positive, the physical and mental channels through which the experiences came would need to be attuned and open to the highest, best sources.

Sometimes parents asked Edgar Cayce for very specific information about the development of their child's psychic abilities. In response, Cayce gave both uplifting encouragement and careful warnings. A number of suggestions were made for helping a child develop his or her intuition. Encouraging natural conversations with the child about the events was one—allowing expression of the experiences and listening to the child's visions, feelings, or intuitive impressions. Parents were encouraged to show normal interest in the experiences but not to place undue emphasis on them. Another suggestion was to set aside time for dream discussion. Frequently emphasizing the normalcy of intuition rather than the excitement or unusualness of the phenomena was suggested. Keeping a record of the experiences would allow the parent to see patterns and allow the child at a later date to remember what the experiences were and how they had been helpful. Telling or reading stories about others who had psychic abilities would encourage a child to develop positive feelings about his or her own experiences.

Also encouraged was the parents' own work on spiritual disciplines, thereby setting a good example for the child. Activities for the parents, such as clarifying a spiritual ideal, setting regular meditation and prayer times, and reading uplifting and spiritual literature, were suggested. The idea was that as parents began to grow themselves, they would find that they were better able to guide their child.

As Cayce said, wouldn't everyone want one's child to become acquainted with his or her Maker and be on speaking terms with the cosmic forces? So how should one develop the psychic forces? Through spiritual living! "So live in body, in mind," said Cayce, "that self may be a channel through which the Creative Forces *may* run . . . so make the body, the mind, the spiritual influences, a channel—and the *natural* consequence will be the manifestations." (5752–2)

Part
Four

17

Edgar Cayce and the Fifth Root Race

*D*uring his lifetime, Edgar Cayce indicated that a new "root race" of souls was beginning to incarnate—individuals with deeply ingrained memories and powers of consciousness from former lives. From his readings it was clear that these children were to bring memories primarily from two sources: Atlantis and Lemuria. However, one of the things that the Cayce readings made clear was that, in contrast to our modern habit of identifying countries by their geographical location, the inhabitants of these two ancient continents took their names from the original leaders of the tribes who peopled expansive areas of those lands. Thus the incoming children could be seen as either children of Atlan or children of Zu.

According to Cayce, Atlan was one of the great leaders on the continent later known as Atlantis. Cayce gave information to a number of
individuals that they had been members of the household of Atlan or
part of the Atlan land and peoples.

One reading informed a man that he had worked with the legendary
Ra in the building of not only the Great Pyramid but also various archi-
val passageways and vaults under the Giza plateau. He was also told
that he would be given the opportunity to help reopen those same
passageways through a similar consciousness in the future, along with
"El-ka [?], and Atlan. These [individuals] will appear." (378-16) This would
happen, said the reading, following a time of "regeneration in the
Mount, or [when] the fifth root race begins." (5748-6) Cayce indicated
that those that were left as guards in the passageways could be passed
only through the high mental attunement of a consciousness similar to
the one that this man had known in Atlantis. Once this high level of
consciousness had again been attained, then the archived records of all
humanity's history would be found.

On the other side of the globe, on the Pacific continent of Lemuria,
the tribe whose first great leader was named Zu lived in a vast land area
that included everything from what is now southern California to northern China. Cayce told one woman that she had been a member of a
family in the tribe of Zu that had inhabited what is now the western
U.S. coast near Santa Barbara, California. Another individual was told
that she had been one of the descendants of Zu who had lived in the
Gobi land, or Mongolia. What is now the United States was called "the
Zu [section] of . . . Oz" (980-1), since families from the tribe of Oz inhabited areas in both North and South America.

Modern-day natives of Hawaii who have studied their peoples' history are aware that they are said to be descended from inhabitants of a
former Pacific island known as Mu, a land that many natives guess to
be Tahiti or some island close to it. According to the Cayce readings, Mu
was a son of Zu. Zu himself was a powerful yet peaceful leader who
became known worldwide for his spiritual wisdom and his ability to
relate closely to the Creative Forces, or God.

Cayce traced several of his own incarnations from the clan of Zu—
from remnants of this tribal family who traveled westward from

Lemuria to what is now Iran. There a divinely conceived soul known as Ra Ta was born to a virgin daughter of the chieftan. Following the birth, mother and son were disowned by the family group, who did not believe the young woman's story of the immaculate conception of her child. The two fugitives fled, finally finding sanctuary with a different tribe in the Caucasus, where they were welcomed and where the amazingly gifted child was raised. Eventually Ra Ta, as a young man, convinced a group from his adopted tribe to travel with him to Egypt, where they joined forces both with the native people and with Atlanteans who were escaping their crumbling motherland. Here, under the godlike guidance of the Christ, or Hermes, Ra Ta inspired and oversaw the building of the Great Pyramid and other sacred archives on the Giza plateau.

Cayce indicated that the individuals who gathered to work with Edgar Cayce during the 1930s were part of Ra Ta's soul group who had incarnated together again as the first subgroup of a new consciousness that would expand human awareness to unimagined levels, regaining much of what had been possible and useful in Atlantean and Lemurian times.

Cayce said that for these highly evolved individuals, levitation, both physical and spiritual, would again be possible—that a level of awareness similar to what Cayce himself possessed would make it possible for individuals to give, while fully conscious, advice similar to that given by Cayce from a deep trance.

Cayce also said that much preparation was necessary before the world could fully birth this new consciousness. "You expect a new root race," he said in one reading. "What are you doing to prepare for it? You must prepare food for their bodies as well as their minds and their spiritual development!" (470-35)

Another of Cayce's incarnations was that of Uhjltd, a wise tribal leader who lived in Persia, or what is now Iran. Uhjltd's mother was an Egyptian princess descended directly from Ra (as Ra Ta was later called) and his father was a prince in the tribe of Zu. Apparently Uhjltd had specifically sought this union in order to again focus within himself the wisdom and attunement with the Creative Forces that had been brought to earth previously through both Zu and Ra.

As a young man, Uhjltd was trained in the temples of Egypt. Afterward he returned to the Persian desert to become the leader of his entire tribe. Gradually he brought order, peace, and prosperity into the lives of the people of Zu. No longer were they nomadic; under the newly organized tribal councils and with the instigation of groups of protective guides for passing caravans, the families of Zu grew settled and prosperous.

Meanwhile, Uhjltd's brother, Oujida, jealous of his brother's position and power, took it upon himself to raid the country of Lydia, domain of King Croesus, capturing gold and taking as prisoners the king's daughter and the daughters of other Lydian nobles. Oujida took Elia, the daughter of the Lydian king, as his wife, but she killed herself rather than spend the rest of her life with a barbarous nomad.

Uhjltd then traveled to Lydia to make peace with Croesus. There he met Ilya, a young niece of Croesus, who pretended to befriend him but then betrayed him and arranged for him to be captured and imprisoned in a tower. The Lydian army then attacked the families of Zu, throwing the latter into panic and turmoil, and those of the tribe who were not killed retreated to the desert in disarray. From this time onward the tribe remained scattered in factions, unable to draw together again under any one leader.

Meanwhile Uhjltd, in prison, constantly communed with the Higher Forces and gradually genuinely befriended Ilya, who now wanted to know who this holy man was. Eventually Ilya helped Uhjltd to escape, though he was badly injured while leaping to the ground from the tower. Unfortunately, at this point Ilya's part in Uhjltd's escape was discovered, and she and her teacher Irenan were thrown over the city wall amid a rain of stones.

Seeing from a distance that the two women were in dire distress, Uhjltd returned to help them, though it meant great injury to himself from the hail of stones. However, finding his horse still waiting for him, Uhjltd made room for the wounded women on the horse's back and rode away toward home. After the three had traveled for several days, Uhjltd and Irenan were near death from their injuries. Finally the horse stopped near a cave, where all rested and Ilya found water. In the cave, Uhjltd underwent what researcher Kevin Todeschi called a near-death experience and a miraculous healing. (In later years, Edgar Cayce was told that this mystical experience from his earlier incarnation as Uhjltd was the origin of Cayce's ability to access higher spiritual levels while giving psychic readings.) At this time Uhjltd was also granted a vision of the city that would later grow up nearby.

Gradually, as more and more people heard of Uhjltd's great wisdom and healing abilities, the cave and its surroundings became a stopping place for caravans. Slowly the area became populated with tents and families. Eventually Uhjltd and Ilya joined together as husband and wife, and from their union a son was born—Zend. Many years later Zend's own son Zarathustra was to bring a new religion, Zoroastrianism, to the nearby peoples, and in later incarnations, Zend himself would come again as a representative of the Creative Forces, first as Joshua and then as Jesus.

The "city in the hills and plains" that blossomed around Uhjltd and Ilya—Is-Shlan-doen—grew by leaps and bounds. Courts were organized for settling disputes, cooperative systems were set up for growing food, and warehouses were built for storing edibles and supplies. Representatives were chosen for trading with the incoming caravans, and many were trained and sent to other lands as teachers of the Creative Forces. The city became renowned for its wide range of healing arts practices.

For many years the city withstood raids and threats of attack with seeming immunity. Greek forces even infiltrated the city with women sent to entice men away from the prevailing peaceful, higher-minded endeavors. Yet nothing seemed to be a match for the Creative Forces that manifested through the combined personalities of Uhjltd and Ilya. Finally, however, the Greeks were able, through a trusted relative, to entice the couple to visit Ilya's original homeland, and while the couple slept, an assassin murdered them both. At the same time, a powerful Greek army attacked Is-Shlan-doen, killing many of the leaders, scattering the townspeople, and leaving much of the city in ruins. Although it was later rebuilt, Is-Shlan-doen never again approached its previous level of influence. Another era of enlightenment, whose leaders lived close to and were guided solely by the Creative Forces, had ended.

The soul that was Uhjltd came to earth again in 1877 as Edgar Cayce, to fill another special role in history: that of bringing into the modern world an awareness of humankind's desperate need to move closer to the Creative Forces. Cayce indicated that he and those who incarnated with him at that time were the first wave of a new level of human awareness—the first of a much larger group returning to help facilitate humankind's rise in consciousness to a level it had not experienced for many millennia.

Now it appears that this larger group has unquestionably begun to arrive. Will the soul that came to earth as Ra, as Uhjltd, and as Edgar Cayce come again at the present time? Will he, too, be one of the currently incarnating children, in order once again to help draw humankind back into closer relationship with the Creative Forces? Only time will tell. But whether or not Edgar Cayce has chosen to reenter during our time, it is the privilege and responsibility of every individual on the planet who is aware of the presently incarnating group of souls, to honor and nurture them in ways that will help them best to attune to the Creative Forces and to spread their powerful message of love and awareness to all of humankind.

18

Fully Imaging the New Consciousness

*I*mportant literature, from both the past and the present, speaks about a potentially attainable new level of human consciousness and offers at least one common concept across a wide variety of thought. Hindus, Theosophists, and Anthroposophist Rudolf Steiner all foresaw a new level or race of human beings—what Theosophists referred to as the "sixth root race."

As has been shown, a remarkably similar concept was also suggested by Edgar Cayce in several of his readings for individuals and groups, as well as by near-death researcher P.M.H. Atwater in her book *Children of the New Millennium* and by NASA photographer Carole A.P. Chapman under hypnotic regression. All three of these latter individuals have referred to the coming new mind and body—the next level of human consciousness—as the *"fifth* root race." Atwater also uses what she says is researcher John White's term *Homo noeticus* in referring to this new human developmental form and mindset, while futurist Barbara Marx Hubbard calls the new humanity *Homo universalis.*

In addition, certain individuals who are currently incarnate as a transitional group just beginning to manifest the new consciousness have also been called Golden Ones by both Chapman and Atwater, Children of the Blue Ray by futurist Gordon-Michael Scallion, the Blue Race by Atwater, and Indigo Children by Lee Carroll. All of these sources refer to greater and greater numbers of advanced individuals who are now incarnate and to an expanded consciousness growing within humanity that has what Atwater calls "the ability to access the higher mind."

NASA photojournalist Carole Chapman, while under hypnosis to discover where her sudden drastic weight gain had originated, began to speak of her "mission" in this current life as "awakening" a group of individuals incarnate in the world whom she called the "Golden Ones." Writing about these souls in her book *The Golden Ones: From Atlantis to a New World,* Chapman stated that these special individuals would in turn birth a new root race of humanity for whom there were no physical boundaries. Chapman saw images of this new humanity, whom she called the "fifth root race," as able to appear and disappear physically even as infants, and she indicated that they would be perennially closely attuned to the loving power of the great Creative Force that many of us call God.

Sri Aurobindo and The Mother also spoke of this new consciousness as being "beyond the human species" and sometimes referred to the individuals now present in the earth who manifest this consciousness as being at the "superman" level of humanity. Sri Aurobindo said that "when gross matter will be sufficiently transformed, they or others of their kind will receive into themselves the descending great beings from the supramental and thus become the first incorporated supramental beings on planet Earth and in the cosmos . . . " Aurobindo and The Mother said that these highly evolved individuals had come to earth to help all of humankind and hasten the beginning of an entirely new era. Later, Aurobindo and The Mother began to refer to a slightly more distant level of consciousness that they called the "supramental" body or consciousness, "Unity-Consciousness," or the "Mind of Light," in which the human species "will no longer be embodied in the manner of the present animal-human procreation . . . The supramental being, as the incorporation of the Unity-Consciousness which in essence is divine Love, will transpose the world into a higher mode of happiness and well-being."

Although both Sri Aubindro, first, and later The Mother told of experiencing the reception of "supramental" energy into themselves, thus putting them into the "superman" category, their followers were somewhat disappointed to find that neither of these beloved teachers became immune to illness, old age, or death as the followers had expected them to do after their "transformation of the cells." However, The Mother in her later years (she lived into her nineties) stated that the supramental species and the spiritual age would "come almost like a bolt of lightning" when it did finally arrive and that "It is in the year 2000 that it will take a clear turn." Nevertheless, The Mother also said that full manifestation of the supramental era probably would not arrive for several hundred to several thousand years.

Maharishi Mahesh Yogi has spoken extensively about what he calls the "unified field," which appears to be essentially the same reality that Ken Wilber calls "Atman." The Maharishi in particular has expounded on the various levels of consciousness possible to human beings as they rise to full "Unity Consciousness." Of the seven stages of consciousness that the Maharishi has taught about, the final four are states higher than ordinary human awareness. The Maharishi lists these latter four states as Transcendental Consciousness, Cosmic Consciousness, God Consciousness, and Unity Consciousness and says that these states are also described in the ancient Hindu Vedas. According to the Maharishi, Transcendental Consciousness (the fourth level of consciousness) is the experience of what he calls the "unbounded inner Self." (This state may also be what Edgar Cayce called individuality—a much larger context of self-awareness than the conscious waking personality.) Randi Jeanne and Sanford Nidich, followers of the Maharishi, have explained that when, through regular practice of the Maharishi's Transcendental Meditation, the individual can maintain Transcendental Consciousness in addition to waking, dreaming, and sleeping awareness, then the individual has reached the level of Cosmic Consciousness (fifth level), in which there is "the coexistence of awareness of the unbounded [in Transcendental Consciousness] along with awareness of boundaries [in waking consciousness] . . . " Following this development, the next two states of consciousness develop gradually and naturally, as the person's understandings regarding the boundaries observed by the waking consciousness are slowly refined and understood in relation to the unbounded knowing of the true Self. By the time an individual has reached "Unity Consciousness" (the seventh stage), he or she has developed truly infinite omniscience and omnipotence, along with the ability to perceive, value, and act with infinite love. Meher Baba of India, using wording from the Sufi tradition, called this level of enlightenment *Fana-Fillah*, the final dissolution of the individual mind (the false self) into God, and said that this immediately results in what he called God-realization, Self-realization, or the "I am God" state.

The Maharishi's program of mantra meditation (TM) was developed to facilitate heightened awareness, first to the level of Transcendental Consciousness and then to the higher states. His *sidhi* program develops *sidhas*, or individuals operating daily at the level of Cosmic Consciousness and higher. The Maharishi has said that when the square root of 1% of the world's population are *sidhas*—or when the number of meditating *sidhas* on each and every continent equals the square root of 1% of the population of that continent—then a permanent state of world harmony and peace that he calls "heaven on earth" will appear as a result of the "hundredth monkey" effect. Recently the Maharishi initiated a program to develop a cadre of about 80,000 *sidhas* meditating simultaneously around the world and around the clock, to facilitate world peace and the raising of the entire world's consciousness.

Psychologist Ken Wilber has offered the image of a ladder of global human development, based on the premise that the stages through which human infants and children progress both biologically and cognitively are parallel to the evolutionary development of general human consciousness over millions of years. Wilber, however, adds to this what has been called the "perennial philosophy," which states that there exists in the universe an infinite Godhead that is not simply a "big person" but is rather the "ground of all things" or the "nature of all that is." It lies totally embedded within everything that exists; in fact, it *is* everything that exists.

This infinite Allness or Wholeness, says Wilber, is not only the original source of all consciousness but it is also the ultimate culmination and potential of all consciousness. According to the "perennial philosophy," human beings progress along what Wilber calls a "path of transcendence" toward full awareness of the ultimate Oneness. This upward trail is known as the "great chain of being." The path involves first building and then dissolving a series of innate structures within the consciousness—beginning with a consciousness entirely embedded in matter and the physical body, and ending as pure spirit and ultimate wholeness.

Wilber delineates eight levels within the "great chain of being." The first two levels are embedded in the subconscious or prepersonal consciousness. They include Level 1 (nature) and Level 2 (body). The next two levels are areas of self-conscious or personal consciousness. They include Level 3 (early mind or "membership" mind) and Level 4 (advanced mind or egoic/rational mind). The final levels exist within the area of superconscious or transpersonal consciousness. Included in this area are two subdelineations—those of "soul" and those of "spirit." The soul aspect includes Level 5 (psychic consciousness, or shamanistic consciousness), and Level 6 (subtle or saintly consciousness). The spirit aspect includes Level 7 (causal or sagely consciousness) and Level 8 (ultimate or absolute consciousness).

Wilber also indicates that there is an irresistible natural *urge* to follow the "great chain of being" from prehuman subconsciousness to transhuman absolute consciousness. He calls the following of this innate urge "the Atman project," taking the name from Atman, the Hindu name for God that indicates an integral Whole, outside of which nothing exists. It is in response to the irresistible urge toward Atman consciousness that ultimately drives the individual and humanity as a whole to find true answers, spurring humankind's ongoing evolution.

Wilber sees humankind now poised at the upper end of Level 4— "midway between the beasts and the gods." However, says Wilber, ever since the human ego crystallized most completely (during the past 1,500 years) in the upper ranges of Level 4, it has become, and will continue to be, extremely difficult to transcend, because it is so stable and strong.

This, then, is apparently the function of the children of the new consciousness: to transcend Level 4 within themselves and to demonstrate in their own lives the psychic consciousness of Level 5. Like the Maharishi, Wilber also suggests meditation as the primary tool for personal and societal transcendence to the next level of consciousness. However, while the Maharishi teaches passive, restful meditation, Wilber advocates more active kundalini meditation, especially for giving a positive outlet to, and transmutation of, excess male energies. Yet Wilber, too, like the Maharishi, suggests that when a critical mass number of meditators has been reached, all of humanity will be catapulted into acceptance of, and reinforcement of, an entirely new consciousness in which all human beings will be one step closer to their highest evolutionary potential as individuals and as a global society.

Finally, sociologist Riane Eisler has developed in her distinctive study of human history from a feminine viewpoint, a unique view of humankind's potential future which she calls a "pragmatopia." The model for this, says Eisler, lies in the far distant past, in cultures as far back as 9,000 years ago, when most of the earth's communities embodied what Eisler calls "partnership societies."

The hallmarks of this cultural system were (1) the equal standing of women and men, within families, communities, and indeed all society; (2) emphasis on creativity and creative technologies that nurtured, sustained, and enhanced life; (3) interpersonal and group relations based on values that we today would consider soft or feminine—on interconnectedness, peacefulness, compassion, responsibility, and concern for the larger community; and (4) a reverence for and sense of oneness with all of nature.

In complete contrast is our current world societal model, which Eisler calls a "dominator" culture. This system is associated with (1) male gods, (2) domination of male over female energies, (3) violence, destruction, and murder as primary means to acquire and concentrate power, and (4) hierarchical and authoritarian social structures.

Eisler offers hope of the transformation of our present culture through what she calls Cultural Transformation Theory. It is based in several new scientific fields. One of these is sociological action research, which explores how human beings can actively participate in their own cultural evolution. Another is the study across many scientific fields of the dynamics of change. Eisler presents a model of social systems that act as biological and chemical systems do, maintaining and changing themselves in the same ways as other natural systems. She especially relates the potential evolution of social systems to the model of "attractors" within mathematical systems—points of magnetism that impinge on stable systems and allow or create changes within these systems.

Eisler says that social patterns are particularly held in place by spiritual education—through sacred stories and through the ceremonies and rituals that re-create these stories. In creating a partnership culture, says Eisler, these processes are governed by the power of linking or affiliating—a power that enables, nurtures, and creates positively the peaceful well-being of the entire society as well as of all individuals within the society.

Eisler believes that in order to achieve the critical mass necessary for accelerating the entire world into a peaceful, egalitarian partnership society, we must help our children construct huge numbers of new myths, innovative rituals, and fresh artistic, scientific, and spiritual images related to empathy, love, intuition, and responsibility. Teaching our children healthy conflict resolution can transform *any* tension into something *productive* rather than *destructive*. Allocating resources, including advanced technologies, toward all these ends can create a new foundation for a transformed world.

Although Eisler reaches her conclusions from a social science point of view rather than a spiritual one and though she never speaks specifically about raising the *level* of the world's consciousness, nevertheless everything she does suggest—especially about creating new stories, rituals, and images that can become the common resources for an entire society's upbringing—might bring about an *upward* transformation in consciousness as well.

If all the organizations and individuals who are in a practical way working toward the conscious evolution of human awareness to the next higher level (Level 5, according to Ken Wilber) continue to nurture and sustain more and more incoming gifted children, then it would appear that at *some* point in the future—whether in 100 years or in 1,000 years—a critical number of individuals will have reached that level of awareness, and at that moment humanity *en mass* will make a sudden leap in consciousness to a position where we, as a human race, can indeed be called *Homo noeticus* or *Homo universalis.* If, as the Maharishi Mahesh Yogi teaches, that critical number is the square root of 1% of the entire earth's population, then when that number of individuals with Level 5 awareness is reached, the entire world will make a sudden quantum leap into a new mindset, making possible a changed world that will live, love, and teach peace and be truly the long-prophesied "heaven on earth."

Suggested Resources

Books

Atwater, P. M. H., *Children of the New Millennium* (New York: Three Rivers Press), 1999.

Baba, Meher, *Discourses* (Myrtle Beach, SC: Sheriar Press), 1995.

Burns, Litany, *The Sixth Sense of Children: Nurturing Your Child's Intuitive Abilities* (New York: New American Library), 2002.

Callahan, Kathy L., Ph.D., *Our Origin and Destiny: An Evolutionary Perspective on the New Millennium* (Virginia Beach, VA: A.R.E. Press), 1996.

Carroll, Lee, and Tober, Jan, *The Indigo Children: The New Kids Have Arrived* (Carlsbad, CA: Hay House), 1999.

Chapman, Carole A.P., *The Golden Ones: From Atlantis to a New World* (North, VA: Mystic Publishing), 2004.

Choquette, Sonia, Ph.D., *The Wise Child: A Spiritual Guide to Nurturing Your Child's Intuition* (New York: Three Rivers Press), 1999.

Dong, Paul, and Thomas E. Raffill, *China's Super Psychics* (New York: Marlow & Co.), 1997.

Edgar Cayce Encyclopedia of Healing, The (New York: Warner Books), 1988.

Eisler, Riane, *The Chalice and the Blade* (New York: HarperCollins), 1995.

——, *Tomorrow's Children: A Blueprint for PartnershipEducation in the 21st Century* (Boulder, CO: Westview Press), 2000.

Ellwood, Robert, *Theosophy: A Modern Expression of the Wisdom of the Ages* (Wheaton IL: Theosophical Publishing House), 1994.

Gelone, Carolyn, *Teaching for Wholeness: Adult to Child* (Mystic, CT: Mystic Children's Studio), Revised Edition, 1992.

Grace, Raymon, *The Future Is Yours: Do Something About It!* (Charlottesville, VA: Hampton Roads), 2003.

Hart, Tobin, *From Information to Transformation: Education for the Evolution of Consciousness* (New York: Peter Lang Publishers), 2001.

——, *The Secret Spiritual World of Children* (Makawao, HI: Inner Ocean Publishing), 2003.

Hubbard, Barbara Marx, *Conscious Evolution: Awakening the Power of Our Social Potential* (Novato, CA: New World Library), 1998.

Jasmuheen, *Living on Light* (Burgrain, Germany: KOHA–Verlag), 1998.

Jenkins, Peggy J., Ph.D., *Nurturing Spirituality in Children: Simple Hands-On Activi-*

ties (Hillboro, OR: Beyond Words Publishing), 1995.

Kueshana, Eklal, *The Ultimate Frontier* (Quinlan, TX: The Adelphi Organization), 1992.

LaVoie, Nicole, *Return to Harmony: Creating Harmony and Balance Through the Frequencies of Sound* (Pagosa Springs, CO: Sound Wave Energy), 1992.

Marshak, David, *The Common Vision: Parenting and Educating for Wholeness* (New York: Peter Lang), 1997.

Maslow, A.H., *The Farther Reaches of Human Nature* (New York: Penguin Books), 1971.

Melchizedek, Drunvalo, *The Ancient Secret of the Flower of Life, Vol. I* (Flagstaff, AZ: Light Technology Publishing), 1998.

————, *The Ancient Secret of the Flower of Life, Vol. II* (Flagstaff, AZ: Light Technology Publishing), 2000.

Nidich, Randi Jeanne, Ed.D., and Sanford Nidich, Ed.D., *Growing Up Enlightened: How Maharishi School of the Age of Enlightenment Is Awakening the Creative Genius of Students and Creating Heaven on Earth* (Fairfield, IA: Maharishi International University Press), 1990.

Quinn, Daniel, *Beyond Civilization: Humanity's Next Great Adventure* (New York: Harmony Books), 1999.

Redfield, James, *The Celestine Vision: Living the New Spiritual Awareness* (New York: Warner Books), 1997.

Reilly, Harold J., and Brod, Ruth Hagy, *The Edgar Cayce Handbook for Health Through Drugless Therapy* (New York: Macmillan), 1975.

Scallion, Gordon-Michael, *Notes from the Cosmos* (Chesterfield, NH: Matrix Institute), 1997.

Spangler, David, *Parent As Mystic, Mystic As Parent* (New York: Riverhead Books), 1999.

Tinsman, Jennifer Lingda, *Not My Gift: A Story of Divine Empowerment* (Mystic, CT: CPS), 1998.

Todeschi, Kevin J., *The Persian Legacy and the Edgar Cayce Material* (Virginia Beach, VA: A.R.E. Press), 2000.

Twyman, James F., *Emissary of Light* (New York: Warner Books), 1996.

————, *Emissary of Love* (Charlottesville, VA: Hampton Rhoads), 2002.

————, *Secret of the Beloved Disciple* (Tallahassee, FL: Findhorn Press), 2000.

————, *The Psychic Children Speak to the World* (Ashland, OR: The Beloved Community), 2002.

Van Vrekham, Georges, *Beyond the Human Species: The Life and Work of Sri Aurobino and The Mother* (St. Paul, MN: Paragon House), 1998.

Virtue, Doreen, *The Crystal Children* (Carlsbad, CA: Hay House), 2003.

Virtue, Doreen, and Tober, Jan, *The Care and Feeding of Indigo Children* (Carlsbad, CA: Hay House), 2001.

Wilber, Ken, *Up from Eden: A Transpersonal View of Human Evolution* (Boston: Shambhala), 1986.

Media Products

Association for Research and Enlightenment (A.R.E.), Children's Pre-sleep Tape Series: *Staying Happy and Calm* (Audiocassette), (Virginia Beach, VA: A.R.E. Press), 1996.

Cayce, Edgar, *The Complete Edgar Cayce Readings* (CD-ROM), (Virginia Beach, VA: A.R.E. Press), 1971/1993.

Melchizedek, Drunvalo: *Through the Eyes of a Child* (Videocassette), (Flagstaff, AZ: Lightworks Audio and Video), 2000.

Scallion, Gordon-Michael: *Children of the Blue Ray* (Audiocassette), (Chesterfield, NH: Matrix Institute), 1988.

Scallion, Gordon-Michael, and Cynthia Keyes: *Children of the Rainbow* (Audiocassette), (Chesterfield, NH: Matrix Institute), 2000.

Sound Wave Energy: Basic Series (Audiocassette or CD), (Pagosa Springs, CO: SWE), 1994, 1998.

Sound Wave Energy: LifEssence (Audiocassette or CD), (Pagosa Springs, CO: SWE), 1998.

Sound Wave Energy: Mental/Emotional Series (Audiocassette or CD), (Pagosa Springs, CO: SWE), 1994, 1998.

Sound Wave Energy: Physical Series (Audiocassette or CD), (Pagosa Springs, CO: SWE), 1994, 1998.

Sound Wave Energy: Spiritual Series (Audiocassette or CD), (Pagosa Springs, CO: SWE), 1994, 1998.

Web Sites

A Place of Light (Community Center for Psychic Children): www.placeoflight.net

Aquativity: www.aquativity.com

Association for Research and Enlightenment (A.R.E.): www.edgarcayce.org

Chapman, Carole (*The Golden Ones*): www.a-new-world.com

Children of the Blue Ray (Gordon-Michael Scallion):
www.matrixinstitute.com

ChildSpirit Institute: www.childspirit.net

Crystal Children (Doreen Virtue): www.TheCrystalChildren.com or
www.angeltherapy.com/articles/crystal.html

Crystal Children (Steve Rother): http://lightworker.com/ or
www.planetlightworker.com/articles/sharyljackson/article19.htm

EarthWalk: www.earth-walk.net

Eisler, Riane, Center for Partnership Studies: www.partnershipway.org

Enchanted Forest Camp: www.psykids.net or www.childspirit.net

Golden Ones: www.a-new-world.com

Indigo Children: www.indigochild.com

Maharishi Mahesh Yogi—Global Country of World Peace:
www.globalcountry.org

Maharishi Mahesh Yogi—Maharishi School of the Age of Enlightenment:
www.fairfield.k12.us/fairfield/schools/msae/msae.htm

Maharishi Mahesh Yogi—Transcendental Meditation: www.maharishi.org

Maharishi Mahesh Yogi—Vedic City, IA: http://maharishivediccity.net

Melchizedek, Drunvalo: www.spiritofmaat.com or (Flower of Life Research) www.floweroflife.org

Nova Alternative High School (Seattle, WA): www.novaproj.org

Psychic Children of Oz: www.emissaryoflight.com

Psychic Kids (Llael Espaze Maffitt and Nancy K. Baumgarten): www.psykids.net

Rother, Steve: http://lightworker.com

Scallion, Gordon–Michael: www.matrixinstitute.com

Sound Wave Energy (Nicole LaVoie): www.harmonyera.com

Twyman, James: www.emissaryoflight.com

Vedic City, IA: http://maharishivediccity.net

E–mail Addresses

A Place of Light (Community Center for Psychic Children): apolfriends@myexcel.com

Aquativity: aquativity@aol.com

Chapman, Carole (*The Golden Ones*): Carole2012@netscape.net

ChildSpirit Institute, Mary Hart: mhart@westga.edu or Tobin Hart: thart@westga.edu

EarthWalk, Valerie Vandermeer: Valerie@earth–walk.net

Enchanted Forest Intuitive Camp, Nancy Baumgarten: nancy@celestial–dynamics.com (Important: Be sure to include the words "Enchanted Forest Camp" in the subject line of your e–mail!)

Melchizedek, Drunvalo: alllife@theriver.com or Flower of Life Research: merkaba@floweroflife.org

Scallion, Gordon–Michael, Matrix Institute: info@matrixinstitute.com

Sound Wave Energy: Info@harmonyera.com

Other Resources

EarthWalk—guidance, programs, and retreats for families and workers with highly aware children: www.earth-walk.net

Rother, Steve—*Children of the New Earth* (quarterly magazine): http://lightworker.com

Redford, Linda—"The Adawee Teachings" (children's program using Cherokee methods of honoring and valuing): www.honorkids.com

Twyman, James—Beloved Community Mystery School (adults/young adults—eighteen weekly lessons): www.emissaryoflight.com

Twyman, James—Emissary of Love Study Course (adults/young adults—sixteen weekly lessons): www.emissaryoflight.com

Twyman, James—Spiritual Peacemakers' Course (ninety-nine lessons): www.emissaryoflight.com

Twyman, James—SpoonBenders Course for Peace (four lessons): www.emissaryoflight.com

A.R.E. Press

The A.R.E. Press publishes books, videos, and audiotapes meant to improve the quality of our readers' lives—personally, professionally, and spiritually. We hope our products support your endeavors to realize your career potential, to enhance your relationships, to improve your health, and to encourage you to make the changes necessary to live a loving, joyful, and fulfilling life.

For more information or to receive a free catalog, call:

1–800–723–1112

Or write:

A.R.E. Press
215 67th Street
Virginia Beach, VA 23451–2061

BAAR PRODUCTS

A.R.E.'s Official Worldwide Exclusive Supplier of Edgar Cayce Health Care Products

Baar Products, Inc., is the official worldwide exclusive supplier of Edgar Cayce health care products. Baar offers a collection of natural products and remedies drawn from the work of Edgar Cayce, considered by many to be the father of modern holistic medicine.

For a complete listing of Cayce-related products, call:

1–800–269–2502

Or write:

Baar Products, Inc.
P.O. Box 60
Downingtown, PA 19335 U.S.A.

Customer Service and International: 610–873–4591
Fax: 610–873–7945
Web Site: www.baar.com   E-mail: cayce@baar.com

DISCOVER HOW THE EDGAR CAYCE MATERIAL CAN HELP YOU!

The Association for Research and Enlightenment, Inc. (A.R.E.®), was founded in 1931 by Edgar Cayce. Its international headquarters are in Virginia Beach, Virginia, where thousands of visitors come year-round. Many more are helped and inspired by A.R.E.'s local activities in their own hometowns or by contact via mail (and now the Internet!) with A.R.E. headquarters.

People from all walks of life, all around the world, have discovered meaningful and life-transforming insights in the A.R.E. programs and materials, which focus on such areas as personal spirituality, holistic health, dreams, family life, finding your best vocation, reincarnation, ESP, meditation, and soul growth in small-group settings. Call us today at our toll-free number:

1–800–333–4499

or

Explore our electronic visitors center on the
Internet: **http://www.edgarcayce.org.**

We'll be happy to tell you more about how the work of the A.R.E. can help you!

A.R.E.
215 67th Street
Virginia Beach, VA 23451-2061

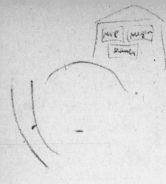

card from Gram
Miraculous Medal + ♥

picture Mike drew +
color pencils.
Pretty dress